Belle
Pearl

by
Arianne Richmonde

Praise For Pearl

"Five stars because Alexandre is worth every one of them."
—*Cindy at The Book Enthusiast*

"I LOVE LOVE LOVE Alexandre! I have been looking forward to reading this book and I can say without a doubt…it was worth the wait!"
—*The Literary Nook*

"I went completely crazy over Alexandre in *The Pearl Trilogy* and I fell even more crazy in love with him in *Pearl*."
—*Books, Babes and Cheap Cabernet*

"Don't miss out on this amazingly hot and smoldering read…you will love it!"
—*Two Crazy Girls With A Passion For Books*

"I devoured this book and loved every second of it."
—*The Book Blog*

"CALL THE FIRE BRIGADE my house is burning down from Alexandre's sexpertise!!"
—*Island Lovelies Book Club*

"This is a MUST READ!!!!"
—*Sugar and Spice Book Review*

"Alexandre is one of my original Book Boyfriends right up there with Fifty… this new look at him only solidified that crush."
—*Mommy's A Book Whore*

About this novel.

Belle Pearl, is the fifth book and the conclusion to Arianne Richmonde's bestselling books in The Pearl Series; *Shades of Pearl, Shadows of Pearl, Shimmers of Pearl and Pearl;* the tumultuous and heart-rending love story between forty-year-old documentary producer, Pearl Robinson, and French Internet billionaire, Alexandre Chevalier, fifteen years her junior.

This book continues from where we left off in *Pearl,* from Alexandre's point of view, and continues the story beyond *Shimmers of Pearl,* so has a *completely different ending* than the trilogy.

As with *Pearl,* there are many scenes in this novel that do not feature in *The Pearl Trilogy.*

At only twenty-five, Alexandre Chevalier is a billionaire. His social media site, HookedUp, is more popular than Twitter, more global than Facebook. With his devastating looks, alluring charm, and his immense wealth, he has women falling at his feet, desperate for his attention—ex girlfriends and an ex-fiancée who simply *cannot* let him go. Although his heart is set on only Pearl, she tests him to his limits and proves that she is even more damaged than he first believed.

Alexandre's dark and dysfunctional past makes him crave a normal relationship with Pearl but he soon finds out that she is not your average woman. However, he believes that they are both two peas in the same dysfunctional pod, made to 'dis-function' together, and is determined to make their union work. But Pearl puts Alexandre in a position where he is made to choose. His loyalties are split, his patience torn.

After many trials, misunderstandings, and revelations of dark secrets, finally their wedding ensues and it looks as if their happily ever after is sealed.

Until something unforeseen rips their world apart.

This is novel #5 in The Pearl Series and is by no means stand-alone.

Reading order:

Shades of Pearl
Shadows of Pearl
Shimmers of Pearl
Pearl
Belle Pearl

About the Author

Arianne Richmonde is an American writer and artist who was raised in both the US and Europe. She lives in France with her husband and coterie of animals.

As well as **The Pearl Series** she has written an erotic short story, *Glass*. She is currently working on her next novel, a suspense story.

The Pearl Trilogy bundle (the first three books in one box set).
Shades of Pearl
Shadows of Pearl
Shimmers of Pearl
Pearl

To be advised of upcoming releases, sign up:
http://ariannerichmonde.com/email-signup

For more information on the author visit her website:
www.ariannerichmonde.com

Acknowledgements

To every one of my amazing readers who demanded more of Pearl and Alexandre. Thanks for all your love and feedback. *The Pearl Series* would not have been possible without you. Thank you to all the bloggers and readers who recommended my books to their friends and followers. Your tireless support and enthusiasm have me in awe. Thank you so much.

Dedication

To Nelle, Angie and Sam; you are always there
when I need you.
Thank you, Nelle, for all your brilliant observations.

Cheryl and Paula, for being my eyes.
To Lilah and The Pearlettes—thank you for being
such a great team.

1

It's true what they say about muscle memory; that your body instinctively does whatever it has been trained to do, seemingly without your brain being involved.

Because right now, my brain was in a fuzzy haze. My limbs felt like the puppet, Punch, being left in a tangle of strings and broken joints, abandoned by his puppet master—gone for a coffee break. My arms were still above my head, tied tightly together. I lay there, all askew, my body in fragmented pieces, but my cock like a thick, solid, wooden rod. Laura's breath was heavy in my ear, her skin oiled and sweet as she sniffed me, her hand clamped about my dick, aiming it inside her.

"Oh yeah, Alex, I've been fantasizing about this for years. In my bloody wheelchair, in my bed, dreaming of you instead of James. Oh darling, I've been waiting for this moment."

My leg kicked up and over her as if it belonged to someone else, not me. I watched it with fascination, curl its way in front of

Laura's chest, not kicking her, but the force of it pushing her off balance, knocking her hand out of its vice-like grip, freeing me from her tight hold and pushing her sideways off the sofa. She tumbled onto the floor.

"Fuck you, Alex! What the fuck? That bloody hurt!"

I tipped my head forward and brought my arms in front of me but my neck instantly fell back into the soft, feathery nest of silk cushions. I'd never felt more uncomfortable about being comfortable in my life.

Laura lurched her skinny body back on top of me. "Not so fast, Alex, I want to get my money's worth out of this Viagra!"

So that explained my erection! Again, I tried to shout and scream but only groans emanated from my cotton-wool mouth.

"I know, baby. I know. You think you have to be all Mr. Faithful to that silly American tart, but we know very well that your lusty relationship won't last, so why not nip it in the bud now, eh? You'll thank me later for this, I swear."

"Laoor....ra."

"I know, darling, I know." She gripped her knees about my hips, spat on her fingers and smeared them inside herself for lubrication. So much for her being turned on. This wasn't about love or lust; Laura had other plans, obviously. She spat on her fingers once more, and spread another glob of spittle where she felt she needed it most, thrusting her skinny frame over me, covering me like a blanket. My arms pushed forward, pressing on her collarbone. I didn't want to hurt her, I just wanted her *off* me. I saw that it was electric cable tying my wrists together. In an infallible sailor's knot.

She tumbled backwards and cried out. "Alex! Ouch!"

"Fuck ow, Laoara," my tongue managed. *Fuck off, off of me!* I pinned her down with my torso so she was locked beneath me.

She grinned as if she had won a prize. "Ooh, sexy, I like a bit of rough. Come on then, Mr. Stud, give it to me, ram it in me, baby!"

My breath was uneven. My heart pounding out of sequence. Jesus! What the hell had she put in that Bloody Mary, apart from Viagra? Qualudes? Some sort of date-rape drug? Enough to bring a horse to its knees, anyway.

We lay there panting, her arms draped about my neck, holding me close to her, her legs hooked about my calf muscles and she thrashed her groin up at me, her hands grappling, trying to find their way back to my dick. But I pressed myself even closer so there was no space between us. I almost wanted to laugh the situation was so absurd. There was something comical about Laura, and in that moment, I remembered the fights we used to have which would always end up with make-up sex and then us laughing about it afterwards. She would goad and provoke me, knowing that the only way we'd even end up speaking to each other again was after we'd fucked.

"Oh Alex, oh Alex, how I've missed this," she breathed into my ear. "You and I are destined to be together. Destined. I love you, darling."

No you don't, you nutter! "Laaoura."

If I moved from my position, she could get leverage again and I couldn't risk it. I wanted to call for help but then realized how mad it would seem. A big grown man like me being 'raped' by a beautiful ex-model? *Yeah, people would really believe that one.* My hands fumbled in front of me, trying to cup my dick to protect its 'virtue.' No, 'cup' is the wrong word, as it could not be cupped—it was like a fucking missile.

My tongue tried to wrap its way around a simple sentence: "Laaoora, pleathe."

She started inhaling me again, writhing beneath me, edging her way higher so my missile was in the perfect spot to be fired into her. "Oh yeah, Alex. Oh yeah, just a couple of centimeters lower...come on baby, give it to me."

And my dick was tempted. How do you undo centuries of male instinct? I wasn't made of stone. Except...I was—my cock, anyway. The drugs were now making me horny too. I half wanted just to fuck her and get it over with, but even in my woozy state, I knew that it was just the beginning of something more ominous. If she got away with this, who knew what was next on the cards? Besides, I was engaged to another woman. Being a cheater wasn't my style, even if I was being coerced into it.

No. Laura isn't fucking getting her insane way with me!

Except she was. Almost. I could feel her pussy poised at the crown of my cock, now soaked with her spit.

Using the arm of the sofa to maneuver myself, I pushed myself down the sofa so my head was now on her chest. My cock was free. For the moment, anyway.

"Oh yeah, baby, suck my tits, that's good."

I thrashed my head from side to side, fumbling with my butter-fingers to untie the electric cable which was digging into my wrists. But it was useless. So I dipped my head over the edge of the sofa and performed a very ungracious somersault, crashing into the coffee table—glasses and Bloody Marys tumbling to the floor—but I managed to roll myself forward with enough force that I landed on my feet in a crouch. Laura's arms slapped into my thighs as she tried to bring me down again, her hooky nails clawing at my jeans, which were half way down my thighs. But I leapt to my feet. At last, I was upright.

Stars flooded my brain as dizziness threatened to topple me over again. My head rushed with a mélange of bright colors, swirling about in dashes and flashes. I could hear Laura cackling hysterically.

You think this is funny, eh? I tried to say without words forming, just moans. But to my horror, I too, was laughing—my belly contracting in painful howls. The drugs were coursing through me. I was now doubled-up. In that second, it was as if every hilarious movie, book, play and memory was crashing into me, making me roar with uncontrollable mirth.

"You see how we're made for each other, darling? That American just doesn't have your sense of humor! No American does. They're so bloody earnest, so goody-goody. You and I are a real *team*, Alex. We're naughty, irreverent, *wild! We* break the law, *we* will stop at nothing."

I howled with hilarity at every word spoken. It was true: *Pearl is a good person. Too good for me. Too wholesome. Too honest. I'm bad. Rotten inside. Killed people. Done illegal deals with Sophie, smuggling gems and all sorts of other moneymaking schemes to get rich and powerful. Pearl deserves better. I deserve Laura. Laura knows how fucked-up I am and she still doesn't care.* I tried to button up the fly of my jeans, my wrists tied, my fingers hopelessly numb. I screamed with laughter at my ineptitude.

"Let's have another drink," suggested Laura.

I burst out laughing again. The idea that she was about to mix another Bloody Mary, lacing it with another round of drugs, was the funniest thing I'd ever heard in my life. I held out my wrists. "Undooo," I howled.

"You want me to undo that sailor's knot, darling?"

I nodded.

"Where would the fun be in that? You know very well that if I undooooo you, *I* will be undone. I think we should get back on the sofa, don't you? One more try and if it doesn't work, I'll mix another cocktail."

A cocktail of drugs. Hmm, not so amusing. My pulse was pounding in my ears. This woman could kill me! I took a deep breath and staggered towards the door. I needed air but not just air—I needed my freedom.

In my peripheral vision—a blur of flesh and limbs—I saw Laura race after me. I kept going, my heart like an old-fashioned steam train, pumping as hard as it could to gain momentum. Laura rugby-tackled me but I stepped aside and she went flying on her face. Her arms curled about my ankles but I kept moving—Laura was letting herself be dragged behind me. I dared not bend down to unlatch her, in case I lost my balance again.

"Where the fuck are you going!" she yelled. It was not a question but a command.

The scenery of paintings, smooth walls and light fittings of the hotel penthouse swam before my eyes as I lugged myself, and the limpet on my leg, to the door. Finally I reached my destination, my head flopping against the wood. I turned the handle and poked my head outside. I wedged my foot in the door and edged my body into the corridor.

Sophie was standing right there.

With Indira.

"We came by to see if you wanted to have tea with…" Sophie stopped herself mid-sentence.

Indira smiled at first, then her eyes swept down to my crotch. I followed her gaze and saw that my missile dick was poking out of my unbuttoned jeans. My hands were still tied with electric cable and groans and moans were coming from my ankles: Laura.

Indira pushed the door with a mighty thud, and Laura cried out:

"Ouch, that's my head, thank you very much! What the fuck—"

Indira's eyes scanned down to the floor where Laura was sprawled out, naked, still clinging onto my ankles.

"Jesus," Sophie said, speaking in French. "What the hell is going on?"

"Help me!" I mouthed silently. "Take Laura away, call James." But I started laughing again, clutching my stomach with bellyache howls.

Indira's hand came down hard on my face. The slap stung like twenty wasps biting me all at once. "You slut! And into dirty bondage games to boot! You disgust me!" She spat in my face and shuffled away, nearly tripping over her flowing sari. I knew what really irked her: that she had wanted to experiment with bondage one time, and I wouldn't play ball.

I rubbed my face against my shoulder to wipe off her spittle. I'd had enough female saliva for one day.

I said with a silent growl, "Sophie, please, help—it's not funny," but between a racing heart and hitched breaths, I chortled again with another round of hysteria, tears streaming down my face, my jaw sore with all the grinning.

Sophie stood there, glaring at me, her eyes two empty holes, her lips twitching.

Like a scolded schoolboy sent to a corner, her disdainful look made me roar all the more.

2

As the drugs wore off, my amusement at the situation waned. Although, the more I thought about Laura, the more I sort of admired her gusto. I had to give her an A+ for effort. But I felt as if I was wrapped up in a psychological suspense movie with the mad ex stalking me, and if I wasn't more vigilant I could wind up dead, poisoned in a back alley somewhere, Laura weeping over my dead body; the body she'd topped off.

One thing was for sure, though: you had to give her ten out of ten for an active imagination.

Once again, my sister had bailed me out of trouble. Indira stormed off in a huff and Sophie rescued me, untied the sailor's knot, and sent Laura on her way, waiting patiently while she got dressed, but not leaving my side until Laura was safely out of the hotel. Sophie called James but he still wasn't answering his cell, or returning calls.

Once I was alone again, and with my dick still Viagra-hard, I called Pearl for some Skype sex–I had to do something to tone down my raging erection. My libido was hungry enough as it was; the last thing in the world I needed was bloody Viagra—I didn't know how long the effect would last but I needed a release.

Pearl was in the bath with the soundtrack from the beautiful 1960's film, *Un Homme et Une Femme* in the background. She wanted to chit-chat about this and that—her meeting with Samuel Myers and how they'd got the gay actress Alessandra Demarr on board, and that they'd be working together on this feature film Pearl was producing, *Stone Trooper*. I wondered if Pearl would be tempted by a gay woman? After all, her first orgasm had happened with her schoolgirl friend.

I didn't want to talk about the film; I needed a release. And fast. I conjured up girlie images of Pearl and Alessandra together, sucking each other's tits—anything to get my wooden dick to climax and then get back to normal.

"I know you have a penchant for pretty women," I breathed into my iPhone as I gazed at the screen; Pearl's beautiful breasts lathered with bubble-bath foam. "Remember when you told me about your first time? When your best friend stroked you with a feather? Fuck," I groaned, my hand moving up and down my mammoth cock. I had Pearl's wet pussy in my mind's eye, me licking her, flicking my tongue on her clit, fucking her hard. Her squirming beneath me as I thrust myself in and out of her slick wet warmth.

"I'd love to suck your cock right now." Pearl was holding her iPad, her big blue eyes staring at me as if she were right there in the flesh.

I curled my grip harder about my erection, jerking my hand up and down vigorously. "Tell me, baby. Tell. Me. How. You'd. Suck. My. Hard. Cock."

"I'd take your big, beautiful centerpiece and guide its silkiness all over my face, licking off your pre-cum, dancing my tongue on your huge, thick crown."

"Oh, yeah…oh baby…" My hand clenched harder, pressuring my swollen tip.

"I'd breathe in the smell of you, Alexandre…the one thousand percent pure, unadulterated, all-male, luscious helping of Alexandre Chevalier."

I flinched at the word 'unadulterated' and wished it were true—wished what had happened to me as a boy hadn't been real. I focused on her other words, 'luscious helping' and imagined myself being served up at some banquet. I started laughing manically again—the drug laugh—taking my phone away from my face so Pearl couldn't see my crazy eyes; the mad Frenchman who wanted her to be his bride.

"Go on," I urged, trying to make my voice sound serious.

Her mouth was pouting and I imagined my cock deep inside it. She continued in a whisper, "I'd tease my lips along your balls and let my hot tongue flick up and down along your rock-hard, thick, throbbing cock, thinking how it makes me come when it fucks me so hard—every time. Every single time. No man has ever been able—"

"Don't *ever* put the idea of another man into my head," I interrupted her. "I don't want to know who's touched you. I don't ever want to even *imagine* that you've been with anyone else. You're *mine*, Pearl. Do you understand? You're fucking well *mine.*" My eyes flashed like two balls of fire, my jealousy surging through my veins in an emerald-green rush.

She was moaning, pleasuring herself, turned on by my outburst. For some reason, she liked it when I showed jealousy. Her iPad was all skewwhiff, balanced precariously amongst a pile of scented soaps and fluffed-up towels—maybe it would end up tumbling into the bath again. It had happened before.

"Tell me about my cock in your mouth," I growled. "About how you can't live without it, that you can't live without me fucking you, fucking your hot, tight, juicy cun—" I stopped myself "—pearlette—"

"It's so sexy, so virile, so huge, and even after that big bad boy has spurted into my mouth, he's ready for round two."

"Round three, round four," I moaned. The truth was that I could have fucked Pearl all day, every day, but I knew neither she, nor any normal woman, could have taken that much of me. I looked down at my cock. It was still swollen as fuck. "When I get back tomorrow, Pearl, I'm going to lick that clit, tunnel my tongue deep inside you, reach your G-spot with my tongue, turn you over and fuck you so hard…"

I tightened my grip, racing my hand up and down my erection until the heat rose within me, my orgasm catching up with visions of Pearl's tight pussy, hugging and climaxing all around my cock, me fucking her hard from behind and coming, fucking her mouth and coming, and in my deep, dark, secret fantasy—shamefully buried and snuffed out from my conscious mind—easing my cock very, very slowly into the forbidden part of her where I would never venture. Off limits. Not allowed, even though she'd suggested it several times.

Somewhere I dared not go because of what had happened to me. The shame. The fear. The humiliation. I had the scar to prove it really did take place that wintery morning at dawn; right there in the crack of my ass.

He was a monster, no doubt.

My mother had done the right thing.

By the time I was on my way back home to New York, very early the next morning, my dick had calmed down and my grin had changed from inane to sober, my jaw still aching from all the laughing, though, and my mind active on how I would need to keep this whole crazy episode quiet.

Very quiet.

The last thing I wanted was for Pearl to find out I'd been bound and drugged, especially by Laura of all people.

For one thing, it did little for my manhood. A black-belt in Taekwondo being nearly overtaken by a skinny blonde with a handful of drugs? It made me look like a real pussy.

Not to mention the fact that Pearl wouldn't believe me for a bloody second. Even my own sister doubted me when I told her the story. There was no way Pearl would be convinced.

This winter wedding business was threatening to undo me. It was still only October. The sooner Pearl and I were married, the sooner all this backlog of ex-nutters would be off my case, out of my life and leave me in peace.

Surely they wouldn't hound a married man?

Little did I know, at that point, that Laura's shenanigans were just the beginning.

I found Pearl in bed. I slipped in beside her and needed, oh yes, I really *needed* to be inside her. Her velvet cave was becoming my security. My home. It was where I belonged and where I constantly wanted to be. I felt secure there.

I didn't fuck her hard, and ravage her as I'd threatened to in our Skype call. No. I held her close, kissing her toothpaste-fresh mouth, my tongue exploring hers with tiny, fluttery movements so I could feel every nuance, every miniscule touch. I entered her wetness, stretching her open, my hands clasped greedily beneath her round ass, bringing her closer with every thrust as she moaned under me.

"Please don't stop, Alexandre," she told me, tears sparkling in her eyes.

"I'll never stop fucking you, baby," I groaned into her mouth. "Never."

She'd got the hang of it, all right. These days, orgasms were coming out of her like a string of pearls. I could feel her now, massaging her clit against the root of my thick dick in a rhythmical rocking movement. I sensed the heat build inside her, her pussy clamping around me, owning me. I couldn't get enough of her. Each time she came, it was more intense, deeper—even more carnal than the time before.

The pair of us were insatiable.

Pearl was truly addicted to me. Couldn't get enough of me. Or my cock.

Or so I thought.

A rude awakening was about to prove me dead wrong.

3

I started noticing the change within Pearl after her first dream. She was crying out in her sleep, tossing and thrashing in the bed, the small of her back soaked with sweat.

"Get off me. You fuck!" she screamed.

I woke up with a start, thinking Rex had jumped on the bed, landing in a painful bound on her breasts (as dogs and cats tend to do), but her eyes were closed and Rex wasn't there—he had his own bed. My hands held her wrists to try and calm her, but it made her yowl even harder and sent her into a kicking frenzy. Her swim-toned legs were strong, crashing against my calves with all her might. *Jesus, what was the nightmare that had caused this?*

"Pearl, chérie, wake up!"

Her eyes flew open. She was panting; beads of sweat were gathered like raindrops on her brow, under her arms, behind her knees.

"Baby, what's wrong? What the hell were you dreaming

about?" I asked, holding her close. But she shoved me away, a sneer etched on her lips.

"I'm going to take a shower, I'm drenched." She tried to smile at me but it was obvious I had done something terrible to her in her dream and she hated me in that instant.

"Baby?" I tried again, taking her hand. But she shooed it away, wrestling herself free from the confines of my embrace.

"Please, Alexandre. I just need a shower, I'll be fine."

"What were you dreaming about?"

Her eyes flashed with fury. "Nothing. Really, I can't even remember. I was being chased by a sort of scaly-fish monster or something. Just a typical bad dream, nothing more."

Liar.

Meanwhile, Sophie had suddenly decided that Pearl was marvelous. She was almost obsessed with her, wondering why Pearl was spurning her friendship.

"Because," I said, "you've been a bitch to her in the past and she doesn't trust you an inch." We were sitting at a bar in a restaurant in SoHo, waiting for our table, listening to *Lady Grinning Soul* by David Bowie. It reminded me of Pearl.

"But I'm getting her a bloody Zang Toi wedding gown—it's costing a fortune!"

"If there's one thing you need to know about Pearl, Sophie, it's that she doesn't give a toss about money. She does appreciate the thought, though, but she's suspicious of your motives, and I don't blame her."

"What, just because I called her a cougar?"

"You called her worse, if I remember. And when you came to dinner the other night you were being all bitchy. Pearl noticed, believe me."

"That was not directed at Pearl but at you, dear brother…my jibe about the engagement ring. You could have had *our* diamond if you wanted it so badly, not buy that second-hand gem that belonged to some Russian royalty who fucked horses."

I laughed. "You were guarding that silly Indian diamond like a phoenix, Sophie. And the vintage piece I bought for Pearl and had converted into that spectacular, eat-your-heart-out-Liz-Taylor ring, I would hardly describe as 'second-hand.' It belongs in a bloody museum."

"Anyway, Pearl is an enigma. She makes me…I don't know…I feel—"

I nearly spluttered my beer all over the bar. "Jesus, you don't *fancy* her, do you? Lay off; Pearl's *mine.*" This place made great Bloody Marys but I'd be steering clear of *those* for a while, so I'd settled for an ice-cold beer.

Sophie cackled with laughter. "No, but I do have to say I think she really is very beautiful. She has an angelic face. Really, she looks like an angel in a Botticelli painting. There's an innocent soulfulness about her eyes. There *is* something special about her. I just wish she wanted to be my friend."

"Give it time, Sophie. Pearl's like a cat. You have to let her come to you; not be pushy or she'll run away."

"By the way, speaking of felines, Claudine called me," Sophie told me. "She says she's left several messages and you haven't got back to her. She's very upset. I mean, *really* upset. Hurt feelings.

You'd better get in touch."

Oh no. "What does she want?"

"Well, she split with her boyfriend recently."

"Oh God."

"She's doing well, though. She's just been offered a campaign by L'Oréal. You know, the glamorous older model, the over thirty type of thing. She looks amazing for her age. She's quite a stunner."

"If you're into bones that look as if they can snap in two and skin paler than alabaster, yes, she's a beauty."

"Anyway, you'd better call her because she's been really bugging me about seeing you. She says she misses you and wants to hang out. She sounded very depressed, very doomsday about everything, despite her modeling success."

I could feel my insides churn. Would there never be an end to this slew of exes battering at my door?

"I'm getting married, Sophie. I don't want to see Claudine. Nor Indira, nor Laura. Nor any other beautiful ex that might pop out from under the fancy wood paneling."

Sophie laughed again and said in English, "It never rains it pours. I love that expression."

I felt my lips tighten. *Bloody Claudine. I thought I was off the hook.* "I'm in love with Pearl," I enunciated—to myself as much as to my sister. *I won't be roped into a guilt trip noose about my neck again. Claudine needs to sort her own fucking issues out with men. There is no way I'll partake in any more mercy fucks for Claudine.*

Sophie dabbed her lips with a hint of gloss. "Alessandra will be all over her, I just know it."

"Who?"

"Alessandra will be all over Pearl."

"That's right, you met Alessandra Demarr, that time backstage after we'd been to see her in that play. I'd forgotten about that. What's she like?"

Sophie turned her face away from me and said, "Oh look, our table's ready. I'm starving, aren't you?"

At the time I didn't put two and two together.

The dreaded phone call came the next day.

"How did you get my number?" I asked Claudine. She hadn't even spoken but I suspected it was Claudine because of the weighty silence that I knew I was expected to fill. Responsible, as I was, for her misery. *Not.*

"Alexandre, I'm so down. My boyfriend and I—"

"I know," I cut in. "Sophie told me. I'm sorry it didn't work out but don't lose hope—there are plenty of other men out there who would be delighted to date you." *Delighted until enlightened…to the psycho side.*

"You're the only man I've ever known who knows how to fuck me properly, Alex."

Uh, oh. "You're being dramatic. Don't be silly."

"I've been on a binge. I've fucked eight men in eight days and not a single one of them has gotten me even close to feeling turned on, let alone having an orgasm."

"Claudine, that's not the way to go about things. Men usually don't care if a woman comes or not. They're in it for themselves. That's why you need to develop a *real* relationship with someone.

19

So he cares about your needs."

"I tried. You think I didn't try? My last boyfriend. But it was a disaster in the end. Even *he* was crap in bed."

I sucked in a deep breath. "Look, I'm sorry but I can't help you. What I can do is pay for you to see someone. A psychiatrist or a counselor—someone you can discuss all this with you in depth."

"All those bloody book boyfriends don't help."

"What?"

"I feel so *inadequate*. All the women in those stories come in thousands of different positions as easily as if they were brushing their teeth. They even come on command. On command for fuck's sake! All the guy has to say is, *'Come* for me baby,' and the woman comes, one point zero seconds later. Just like that! As fast as clicking a finger. Is that even possible for a woman? Because it sure as hell isn't possible for me! I can't come at all, let alone on bloody command. What's wrong with me?"

"Claudine, that's fantasy, not reality. In reality things are more complicated. Don't believe what you read. I know…my mother's into that shit. You think if all women were coming on command they'd be reading those books? No, they'd be busy fucking instead."

"It's not just the novels but the magazines, too. It's all about the men. How to please *the man*. How to be a sex goddess. What about *us?* Why aren't they being taught how to please *us?*"

I thought of Sophie. This was her next business plan—to set up a 'romance spa' as she described it. Very chic. Expensive, where men would be trained to please women—women would be the only clientele—no male clients allowed. The sex workers cum 'escorts' (yes, the word cum is very appropriate here) would be handpicked. Models—really good-looking types who would learn everything from scratch. Have their bad habits wiped clean. Learn how to make a woman come from just a foot massage. How to give her mind-blowing orgasms, even if she'd never experienced one before. There would be sex workers to accommodate gay women too. It would be fantasy haven. But better than fantasy, fantasy made reality.

"Alex? Are you there?" Hell..ooo?"

"Yes, Claudine, I'm still here. I was just thinking about my sister's business plan, sorry. Listen, I'm serious—I'll pay for a shrink or someone you can talk to, but I can't see you myself. I told you I was serious about Pearl. We're getting married."

"But you're not married *yet?*"

"As good as. We're engaged."

"But you haven't got a ring on your finger."

"Claudine—"

"Which means you're still *technically* single."

I took another deep breath and looked at my bare left hand. I wanted that wedding band on my finger more than I imagined Rex wanted a big, fat, juicy bone.

And damn it, I wasn't bloody well going to wait until winter.

4

When Pearl suggested that we go to LA, I jumped at the chance. Her bad dreams had gotten out of control but she wouldn't discuss them with me, just insisted she couldn't remember what had happened each time. Yet I could feel her pulling away. Her desire for me was wavering like a flickering candle. Why all of a sudden? As if something had triggered the bad dreams, which in turn were making her jump when I touched her as she slept. What and why?

I wondered if I was somehow responsible; if I'd been too sexual with her—too dominating, too insatiable. She was holding something back but I had no idea what. So I put it down to the documentary she and Natalie were making on child trafficking. The tales she told me of young girls being raped and beaten were pretty horrific. Selfishly, I was glad that Pearl wanted to take a break from making controversial documentaries and move into something less harrowing: feature films. Although, dealing with actors' egos could also be pretty tough, but at least her day-to-day work would be somewhat more lighthearted.

So LA would be a breath of fresh air, I thought. We'd go, take a vacation and then I'd leave her there if she wanted to stay on as I had a business trip in Canada coming up. I hoped that it would calm her down a bit—a change of scenery would stop those nightmares. She could tinker with the *Stone Trooper* script with the scriptwriter, as Alessandra Demarr had insisted on changes. Being a Tony award-winning actress, Alessandra had some clout and Sam Myers seemed to be bending over backwards to keep her sweet.

LA was perfect. Sunny, blue sky, palm trees, people smiling incessantly as if they were taking some sort of happy pill. Our trip was made all the more enjoyable by our choice of rental car: a powder blue, 1960 Eldorado Biarritz convertible Cadillac. It had fins and glistening chrome that shone silver in the sunlight. I felt as if Pearl and I were riding on a giant shark, cruising the wide avenues, spotting other vintage cars and California girls as we sped by, the wind catching our hair, the music blasting through the speakers. Pearl looked like a true California Girl herself— tanned and lithe, golden and sun-kissed, so I played the song, *California Girls* by The Beach Boys, and we sang along.

We were on our way to Alessandra Demarr's house in Topanga Canyon and when we arrived, my eyes strayed, not to Alessandra in her black negligee outfit, but to her classic car, a 1962 Porsche 356B, also black. As Alessandra eye-fucked Pearl, roaming her saucy gaze lasciviously all over Pearl's body and suggesting Bloody Marys of all bloody things (yes, I know), I was only too glad to take Alessandra up on her offer of taking her car for a spin.

"She's all yours, Alexandre, the keys are under the mat."

"I can see you can't get rid of me fast enough," I said with a wink.

"Come back in half an hour," she said in her lilting Italian accent, taking Pearl's arm and guiding her away.

Pearl looked like a lamb being led to slaughter. Sophie had been right; beautiful seductress Alessandra was all over her. Funny, we could have been siblings, Alessandra and I. She had eyes my color: fiery green. I guess I was used to looking at myself in the mirror and didn't think about my eyes, one way or another, but on Alessandra they looked predatorily unnerving, as if she were about to literally devour Pearl. I wondered if I looked the same. Like a wolf. Or a panther. Because before Alessandra began her feast, I imagined that she'd lick Pearl all over first and taste every inch of her body. It turned me on, actually, to envision this, and I felt rather wicked for leaving my fiancée in her clutches, but it also amused me.

At first.

The drive was beautiful. I took the car along Pacific Coast Highway, speeding, seeing how the old Porsche could handle corners, as the ocean shimmered on one side and scrubby mountains rose above on the other. I figured that if I got stopped, I'd just show the cops my French license—it usually did the trick. No points off because the paperwork was too much hassle.

When I returned, I found the two women snacking, and drinking their Bloody Marys. I wondered for a second if Alessandra had done a Laura on her, as Pearl was innocently sipping her drink through a straw. Alessandra was wet, had obviously gone for a swim; her pert breasts clinging to her see-through dress, her hand on Pearl's thigh. A vision of them kissing flashed through my head. I closed my eyes to think of something else so my hard-on would go away.

Alessandra looked up. "Hi Frenchie."

"Hi, baby," Pearl said. "How was your drive?"

"Beautiful." I stood there, legs astride, watching the two of them.

"I was just trying to persuade your fiancée to stay on as we need to work on the script."

I knew it. She was going to get her smooth, gay fingers all over Pearl. For a second, I felt a frisson of jealousy tingle through my spine. I stared Alessandra down. *She's mine, bitch-on-heat.* I walked over to stake my claim. I put my hands on Pearl's shoulders and kissed the nape of her neck.

I'd test Pearl, I decided. If she wanted to stay…well then…she'd get seduced and she damn well knew it. She'd have to battle with her inner-gay-goddess all on her own. If she came home with me, then she really was my girl. I couldn't make that choice for her.

"Stay, chérie, enjoy the weather, have some *fun* with Alessandra," I said with a wry grin. "Anyway, I have to go to Montreal for a meeting so you might as well hang out here for a bit."

"I don't know," she wavered, looking at Alessandra and then at me. "I should really get home, but it *is* so beautiful here; so nice to feel the sunshine on my back."

"You're staying, Pearl," Alessandra barked like the alpha female she was. "I won't allow you to leave yet. We have important
work to get done here with the script."

I almost wanted to take the two women at once and fuck
them both, there and then. Show Alessandra who was boss. I was
also extremely turned on thinking about them together. My heart
raced just imagining our threesome, but I knew it would be a very
bad idea. Pearl would go wild with jealousy, and anyway, it would
feel like incest; Alessandra was too similar to me.

What would happen, I wondered, if Pearl was truly gay,
though? If she played around with Alessandra and got converted?
The woman was every inch a movie star. She had the X factor,
that *je ne sais quoi* that set her apart from the crowd. And she
wanted Pearl. I almost felt like calling Ellen DeGeneres to break
up the happy party… distract Alessandra, get her away from *my*
woman. Insanely, I felt threatened by her. Ridiculous! Being
threatened by a she-wolf when I was the alpha male?

I guess that's why I toyed with the idea of Pearl staying on.
To prove to myself I could handle it. So paradoxically, by not
stopping her and being so blasé about it all, I actively encouraged
Pearl to remain in LA for a few days.

The next morning, while Pearl and I were making love—and I
say 'making love' because it was far more than just a fuck—she
pushed me off her, saying she felt sick. It was sudden. A click-of-
a-finger sudden. One second she was squirming beneath me in

ecstasy, and the next she was repulsed, looking as if she really *was* about to throw up. Was I going crazy? Was this Alessandra Demarr thing for real? *Jesus. Is my woman a fucking full-on lesbian?*

As the day went on, I still wasn't sure what was going on. Pearl thought she had food poisoning. Then I decided that perhaps she was pregnant. *Hallelujah!*

We were walking along the oceanfront by Venice Beach. I could feel Pearl's coolness. Normal, I decided, pregnant women often push their males away—human nature.

"Could you be pregnant?" I blurted out after a long bout of silence.

"I wish," she said in a sad voice. "No, if I were pregnant my breasts would feel swollen and I would have missed my period by now."

"What's wrong then, baby? I get the feeling that you'd rather I weren't around for a while."

"Just that smoothie I drank yesterday, I think."

I was hoping that she'd say, *Don't be crazy, of course I want you around.* Or, *I'm coming back with you, coming with you to Montreal.* But she didn't. She just clutched my arm and walked ahead in silence, her private thoughts ticking away in her head. Not letting me in. Mentally pushing me out. Everything seemed more interesting to her than opening up to me. She people-watched the assortment of nutters that passed us: a guy on roller-skates with a guitar, a bodybuilder wearing a leopard-print leotard, a woman with huge round breasts that looked as if they would pop any second, a dog wearing shades.

"Pearl, are you sure you're okay?"

"It would be nice to live by the ocean, wouldn't it?"

Ignoring me. "Just say the word and we can buy a house in Malibu. Whatever you want. I could surf and you could walk along the beach with Rex, unless you're brave enough to brace the icy water. Would you like that?"

"Maybe." She smiled weakly. Nothing I said seemed to warm her.

"You don't have to keep working, you know. You can throw in the towel with HookedUp Enterprises any time. Be my kept woman. Read novels and laze about in the sun."

"I've worked all my life; I'd get bored. Anyway, what about you? You said you'd break things up with Sophie and HookedUp, yet you still carry on, even though it's obvious she wants to see our relationship come to an end."

The Sophie issue again. Whatever I said, Pearl was convinced that Sophie was out to get her. I kept my mouth shut. I got the feeling that *whatever* I told her, it wouldn't work out in my favor.

"Alexandre, if you and your life met right now, right here, what would you say to it?"

"What?"

"If you and your life could have a conversation, what would you tell it?"

"Je ne regrette rien," I said with a laugh, quoting the Edith Piaf song.

"Seriously."

"I *am* serious. The only thing I might regret is not having kissed you sooner."

"If you could re-live your life, is there anything you'd do differently?"

I tried to gauge her expression but she wasn't giving anything away. I answered, "I am who I am because of all my choices; the good and the bad. Even the mediocre." I thought of Laura and a shiver of shame crept up the back of my neck. "I mean, thank God things happened the way they did, or I might have ended up with Laura and I wouldn't have met you." The second I said those words I wished I hadn't bloody mentioned Laura.

"Do you still think about her?"

Yes. That she's a fucking fruitcake! And I just escaped a bloody close shave. "She's a friend, I guess. We shared a past, that's all." I felt my face heat up.

"So you don't agonize over choices you made and wish that there were things you hadn't done?"

Pearl was onto me. Somehow, *she knew.* That's why she'd cooled off. *Did she know about Laura trying to fuck me?* Or perhaps she'd guessed about my mother? The way she was staring into my eyes had my solar plexus feel as if someone had swung a baseball bat at my gut.

I tried to sound cool. Unfazed. "Sometimes you don't have a choice, Pearl. External forces choose for you."

"We always have a choice. A choice not to get ourselves into bad predicaments in the first place. At least when we're adults, that is. Children don't get a chance to choose."

And was she now *choosing* to break up with me, or something? Her glass-cold face wasn't revealing a thing.

"Your mother, for instance? She had a choice," Pearl went on.

Jesus! What does she know? Does she know what my mother did? "My father was a monster," I said in retaliation, my teeth gritted.

"What happened to your father, anyway?" she asked, her eyebrows raised as if she had guessed the real truth.

"He disappeared," I said, as casually as I could.

"Oh really?" Her brows did their thing again.

"Yes, really, Pearl. That nasty douchebag just disappeared into thin air."

"Aren't you worried that he may come back and *haunt* you?"

I told her that he had disappeared but she seemed to know that he was *dead*. She used the word 'haunt.' *How* did she know? I said in a cold-fire voice. "He's gone for good. He won't come back. Ever."

5

I feel his hands around my shoulders. He's behind me, pressing himself up against my back; his hug tight—he's squeezing the breath from my lungs with his grip. I can smell the whiskey on his breath, like dragon fire, and I wonder what would happen if I lit a match—would his breath go up in flames?

I imagine myself as St. George, piercing this creature—because when he's like this, he IS a creature. Yeah, I could lance this slimy dragon right through his leg. He would roll over in pain. I wouldn't actually kill him but I'd maim him so he could never hurt me again. Because he would truly fear me.

Forever.

I want to move. But I don't. If I move, it'll wake him and he's beginning to snore; the air around us thick with molecules of whiskey, dancing around his smelly mouth. Molecules of hate. And lies. I mustn't hardly breathe. I mustn't make a sound. He'll fall asleep, snoring like a wild hog, and when he's out cold, I'll leave the room.

I want to go to my mother but she's so weak she can't protect me. She can't protect herself. If she cared, she'd do something. Only Sophie cares but Sophie isn't here.

I can hear the snow, softly tapping against the windowpane of my room. I look at the posters on my wall and wish I could escape inside them. Fly in my spacecraft to a different planet and never return. I close my eyes and prepare myself for the cold outside. My parka will have to do. If I walk fast enough, I'll keep warm. There'll be the man selling chestnuts—in a couple of hours. I want to steal some coins from Papa's pockets but he'll hear. Like a bat, he is, even when he's drunk.

Why? The only word now in my head is why.

Why, why, why?

Why does it have to be this way?

I felt something pressing into my back and realized with relief that it was Rex, his paws digging into my shoulders as he stretched out on the mattress, snoring rhythmically. I was about to push him off the bed (when did he jump up?), but a wave of gratitude swept over me, a surge of butterflies swooped about my stomach, knowing that it was just my boy Rex, and I flung my arms about him and hugged him close, kissing his soft ears. I was grateful for every goddamn thing in my life at that moment.

I had escaped. I got away free and clear. Scarred, both mentally and physically yes, but free. Not in a mental hospital somewhere. Not beaten down. Not the speck of dust, the vessel of despair my father wanted me to be. I was a survivor, I *am* a survivor, and like all survivors, we learn the hard way.

I am who I am because of my past. Je ne regrette rien.

However crazy Sophie drove me at times, I thanked her for

everything she had done for me. She gave me my dignity back. She told me I was a hero and deserved to be called Chevalier. She taught me to be strong, and how to fight. She fed me.

I owed her, literally, my life.

I got showered and dressed and took Rex to Central Park. With Sophie on my mind, I called her. I wanted to let her know that Elodie was doing fine; had even been going out with friends, and was dressing less like a Vampire Goth and more like a girl her age. I missed Sophie. We'd been sparring, mostly due to her previous attitude towards Pearl, which, although now over (as far as Sophie was concerned), Pearl was still wary and suspicious. It was going to take more than a wedding gown to patch things up. It was going to take time.

Time…the great healer of adversity.

"Sophie," I said into my cell, as I walked with Rex past Tiffany, casting my eye along the display of jewelry, wondering if I could find a necklace to match Pearl's ring. "How are things in Paris? Have you seen Maman lately?" I don't know why I asked—I knew the answer.

"No, I haven't had time. So many meetings."

"Oh yeah? Anyone I should know about?"

"I've bought a chunk of Myers Industries."

"Myers Industries?"

"Samuel Myers; the one you and Pearl are doing *Stone Trooper* with."

"Well that's a surprise," I said, wondering how this news would go down with Pearl. "What brought that about?"

"He's going broke, Alexandre. He's in dire straits. If someone doesn't bail him out, that movie won't get made."

"Since when have you felt so charitable, Sophie?"

"Not charity, just a good business deal and, you know, looking out for my future sister in-law."

"Have you told Pearl?"

"I think you'd better tell her. Something tells me she might see it as a sort of *coup d'état* if my money's involved in helping produce the movie."

"Yeah, she's proud of her autonomy with this project. I know she wouldn't be too thrilled about you being a part of it. I mean, *I'm* not even involved. I'm not sure how she'll take this, Sophie."

"It's only money, Alexandre. I'm not getting involved in any way creatively. It upsets me that she's so offhand with me. I wish she didn't feel so alienated, so mistrustful. I'd like to be friends. Go shopping, see a movie, you know."

"Just give it time, Soph. Give it time." I moved on, crossed the street and walked toward the park.

"What are you up to right now?" she asked.

"About to go to Montreal. I'm seeing a video games artist there. This new venture could be big, Soph, really big."

"Well, good luck. I know you love that shit."

Despite my reservations about Sophie now being involved with Samuel Myers, I felt a rush of nostalgia pump through my heart—I believed that my sister really did want to make things right with Pearl. It was true; her money would save everyone's ass if Sam Myers really was in a financial bind. "What about you? Are you happy?" The question popped unexpectedly out of my mouth.

"Happy?" Her voice cracked just a touch.

"Well isn't that what life is all about? Finding your slice of happiness? Love? Peace?"

There was silence. I felt bad. I wondered for a second if Sophie had *ever* been truly happy. I had found my little piece of heaven with Pearl. Was Sophie still searching?

"I'm getting there, Alexandre. I'm seeing someone now."

"Oh yeah? Who?"

"We'll see."

"Okay, you don't want to tell me. That's fine. I'm glad you're dating, anyway."

"I'd prefer to tell Pearl, myself—when the moment's right. And I don't want Elodie to know."

"Of course not."

"You know, gay is all very cool and hip, but when it's your own mother? It might not go down so well with Elodie." She sucked in a long breath. "Have fun in Montreal. Is Pearl still in LA?"

"She's hanging out with Alessandra Demarr."

"Hanging out?"

"Tinkering with the script. Alessandra has taken a shine to Pearl—you were right."

"Slut."

"What?" She bloody better not be referring to Pearl.

"Actresses are all the same," she ranted. "Such narcissists. Always seeking attention. Not enough love from daddy or something. They want the world to love them. Anyone will do."

"Pearl's not anyone, Sophie. I can easily see why a gay woman would go potty over her."

"Shut up already!"

"Why does this bother you? You're feeling protective over

35

Pearl?"

"Something like that. Anyway, I must go. My trainer's coming over any minute and I need to get ready."

"Okay. We'll speak soon. Oh Sophie, one more thing…"

"What?"

"This Sam Myers business. You swear it's just your share of money involved in *Stone Trooper*? You promise you won't get involved in the creative side of things."

"I swear."

"Okay, then."

"Bye."

I pressed 'end'. A frisson crept up my spine—a sort of premonition of doom, although I couldn't pinpoint what. I pulled Rex away from the edge of a mailbox—dogs, men, we all want to make our mark—piss on everything; tell the world that this spot, or that, belongs to us. "No, Rex, enough is enough—how come your bladder always has extra to spare? Come on, boy, let's go to the park."

While Pearl was in sunny LA, New York was turning from autumn into winter. Days were passing more slowly; dark evenings were descending more rapidly. Montreal was even worse. The minute I stepped off the plane, I felt the air, icy on my cheeks. Pearl and I had spoken on the phone before takeoff but the line went dead. She said she had something important to tell me—the thing which had been responsible for her nightmares. Finally, she was going to divulge her secret. *We all have secrets and*

that's what a relationship is all about—finding the right moment to reveal pieces of our past. Pearl was about to share hers, but I was still hiding my own slithering nest of vipers in a dark pit. It felt unfair and reminded me that she was too good for me.

Her call came through, and I picked up, feeling a sense of relief. Though her voice was shaking, trembling with rage.

"Why didn't you tell me, Alexandre?"

Heat spiraled through my veins. My mother's secret? Laura's Bloody Mary? "Hey, babe, great to hear your voice. What's up?"

The tirade began. Samuel Myers. Sophie. Shit, I'd forgotten to tell her about Sophie coming on board when we'd spoken yesterday.

"Calm down, chérie, I was going to tell you; it just slipped my mind."

"Bullshit!"

"It's just money, Pearl. No big deal. Sophie won't be involved in any way whatsoever—she's just helping out financially."

The conversation dragged on—Pearl screaming at me, which she had never done before. She was usually so calm but her conversation was laced with threats, tumbling from her livid lips: phrases like 'future ex-marriage' and 'our relationship is over.'

I had to act fast. She was hysterical about this Sophie thing. I said in a level voice, "I'm coming to get you now, Pearl. I'm going to cancel my meeting, hire a jet, and fly straight out to be with you and we'll get married in Vegas tomorrow. You can still have your white wedding but let's just stop this waiting game nonsense and get married."

But she wasn't having it. "You're not listening to a goddamn word I've said, Alexandre Chevalier. Once you have split with

Sophie, once and for all—gotten out of HookedUp, *then* we have a chance of making our relationship work. Until then, adios amigo, because you know what? The last thing in the world I want right now is a relationship with a cock."

I felt like the dragon being lanced by St. George. So *that* was it…she was gay, after all! She'd fallen in love with Alessandra Demarr and wanted me out of the picture. More fool me. What an idiot I'd been to be so casual about the whole thing. Worse, actively encouraging her to explore her inner bloody lesbian!

"Is that all I am to you? A cock?" I said quietly.

"Men are pigs. Pigs! You rape women. Everything you do is conditioned by your dicks." She went on another tirade…something about rape in South Africa, celebrities shagging mentally handicapped children, and men fucking underage girls. She must have been getting updates from Natalie for their documentaries. But Pearl was preaching to the converted. If anyone knew how sick men could be, it was me.

"Pearl, my darling," I said in a gentle voice. "What's suddenly brought all this on? Is it Alessandra?"

Between her sobbing and hitched voice gulping for air, I could hardly understand a word Pearl said. "Call Daisy," she hiccupped, "she'll explain. I can hardly speak right now I'm so furious about Sophie. I do not want Sophie in my life!" She hung up on me.

So we were back to the Sophie topic again. Pearl was all over the place. The hairs on my arms bristled with chilled fear. I was about to lose my Pearl. My *life*. For whatever reason, she wanted me *out* and she was using Sophie as an excuse to extricate herself from me. But I simply wasn't having it. No fucking way.

I called the videographer with whom my meeting was sched-
uled, and cancelled him. And I instructed my assistant to get a
plane to take me immediately to LA; I required a car and he also
needed to book a preacher to marry us in Vegas that very night—
orchestra and all—and a jet to take us away to Bora Bora for our
honeymoon. I'd nip this nonsense in the bud. Pearl and I would
get married and live happily ever after. I'd deal with the Sophie
issue at a later date when I'd got Pearl under control. Because she
did need to be controlled. She was like a racecar spiraling all over
the track. She needed me to steady her. If she'd turned gay, I'd
simply ease her back again into being heterosexual. She'd loved
sex with me before—I'd win her back again. I'd mend her broken
wing; the wing someone had damaged in her nightmares.

I was used to hysterical women. Pearl would be no different.
And even if she were just as nutty as the rest of them, I didn't
care; I wanted her anyway.

I called her back. She would have had time to cool down a
little. "I've cancelled my meeting; I'm on my way."

"Well I won't be around when you get here," she said
through tears.

"Don't be silly, Pearl, just stay where you are."

"I don't want to see you." *The lance, again...stabbing me.*

"Please explain what's going on, baby. Is it Alessandra? Is it
those nightmares you've been having? What's going on?"

There was a long pause and she eventually said, "A long time
ago when I was at university..."

Finally the truth. But she stopped mid-sentence.

"Go on, chérie...I'm here for you. I love you. Please share
your pain with me. Your pain is *my* pain—I can get you through

this."

"No you can't, you're a guy and sorry, Alexandre, but males repulse me right now. I am *disgusted.*"

"I understand, baby. I swear, I do. I agree—men can be pigs. I may be a man but all I want is to love you, protect you, and care for you. Please tell me what happened, my angel. You can trust me. I'm here for you."

The floodgates opened. It all came out. The gang rape at college. The spiked drink (well, Laura taught me about the infallibility of that one). How Pearl felt she'd asked for it because she was wearing a miniskirt. The guilt. The sense of culpability, shame, and then the blackout which morphed into a blank-out— memories better left buried.

Oh Pearl, I wanted to say; *I've been there, too.* But I didn't get a chance. I managed to assure her how it wasn't her fault, how we'd get through it together, but she was so upset she couldn't hear me. She started ranting on about Sophie again, then hung up. I called back but she'd put her cell on voicemail. I left several messages, anyway, telling her to meet me at Van Nuys airport where we would catch a private jet to Vegas. Although, somehow, I knew things weren't going to be quite so simple.

I'd have to be the bulldozer guy. I had no choice. Whether Pearl liked it or not, I was coming to get her. She was falling off a cliff with her broken wing and I was the only person who could catch her.

I dozed off on the plane, planning every move in my head: our flash-lightening wedding, our honeymoon, and how I'd insist on us both taking a break from work—maybe that tree-house in Thailand I'd been fantasizing about would be a good plan. Pearl needed a rest, needed time to heal.

August in Paris. Tempers are raising the thermometers even higher.

We had a picnic by the river today and everything was perfect. Sophie's back home from staying at her friend's. Papa's been on good behavior. Maman loves him with every tiny piece of her heart. Smiles; making sexy eyes, laughing, happy dinners, and happy faces. But I can feel the demon returning. The slimy creature is making its way back inside him and settling in for the night. Sophie says he's okay; that he's taken his medication, but I can feel it bubbling under his skin. I hold Sophie's hand. We're watching TV.

I whisper in her ear. "Stay in my bed tonight."

She laughs. "You're a big boy, you don't need me."

I want to tell her how he rubbed himself up against me—when she was away. When he wasn't taking his pills. He rubbed himself up and down, through the sheets, and I could hear him moan when he stopped. I could feel the wetness. He gripped my shoulders. He rubbed. He cried. He rubbed. He got up and left.

"I don't want him rubbing again," I tell Sophie.

She takes my hand and leads me to her bedroom, away from our parents, who are still staring at the TV screen. Sophie isn't smiling now. "What did he do? Did he touch you here," she asks, her finger pointing to her private place.

"He didn't touch me there. But he breathes in my ear and cries and rubs himself up against me. He tells Maman he's coming to say goodnight to me and read me a story but sometimes he falls asleep in my bed when he's drunk."

"The bastard." Her eyes are looking about her as if she's planning something. "And Maman does nothing?"

I nodded my head. "She doesn't know."

"No point telling her because she won't believe you anyway. But I believe you, Alexandre. I know what he does. I know." Tears are in Sophie's eyes now. I wonder if he has rubbed her too, but I don't ask. "Are you going to stay at your friend's house again?" I ask with fear.

"No, I'll stay here tonight. If he touches you, call out to me. Okay?"

I nod my head.

I woke with a jolt. The plane was landing. Pearl and I had more in common than she realized. We were both victims. The only difference was that I was a victim who would seek revenge because I'd grown tough over the years. I wasn't that vulnerable little boy anymore. I'd find out who had hurt Pearl and give them what was fucking coming to them.

The rental car my assistant had organized for me was waiting. I was glad to see it was the latest Mercedes—I'd need something speedy because Pearl was really giving me the runaround—not picking up her phone. I drove to the hotel in Santa Monica where she was still staying. But soon found out she wasn't. She'd bloody well checked out without giving any indication of where she was going. Calling her was fruitless. She was obviously in a terrible state and it seemed she wanted nothing more to do with me, until I, literally, handed her a signed affidavit proving that Sophie and I had parted ways. It was crazy—as if that were something I'd be able to do overnight...a multi-billion dollar company? Pearl should have known better, but then I guessed that working in documentaries and film was a far cry from what I did, and she simply didn't have a clue about how many people it would involve—the logistics of doing such a thing. Pearl was morally blackmailing me: wanting me to choose between her and Sophie, obviously still convinced that Sophie was out for her blood. I could see, too, from Pearl's perspective, why it looked like Sophie was being sneaky. What a fucking mess!

The only place I could imagine Pearl being—unless she'd hightailed herself out of LA altogether—was at Alessandra Demarr's house. Of course, Alessandra wasn't picking up either, but I sped along Pacific Coast Highway toward Topanga Canyon, hoping I'd find Pearl there.

What a fucking fiasco. I had never chased a woman like this before in my life. All that talk about letting women come to you like cats or children, and here I was flying along in this Mercedes in hot pursuit of a madwoman. A fucked-up, dysfunctional, neurotic nutter, just like every other female in my life.

The only difference was that this time I felt that my world was at stake. I needed Pearl and I couldn't be without her. At least, I couldn't be *happy* without her.

The gods were on my side. I spotted Pearl exit Alessandra's driveway, but because it wasn't the same powder blue Cadillac, it took me a second to register. She'd changed her rental car and was now (I was pretty sure it was her) driving a BMW. I did a screeching U-turn and pursued the car. It sped up—a wild driver was at the wheel and I knew, by that point, it was definitely Pearl. Our cars were careening along the highway as if we were in a Steve McQueen movie—I was racing to outrun her. The Mercedes and the BMW...always had been rivals on the road. I flashed my lights at Pearl but it only made her go faster. This was insane; we'd get pulled over by a cop—worse, this was LA, we might have a gun held to our heads or flung on the ground and handcuffed.

I zigzagged like a lunatic, weaving between other drivers to pin Pearl down.

Finally, she pulled over at a restaurant parking lot. I overtook her, and then screeched to a halt. I got out of my car and pelted towards her, just in case she got it into her head to take off again. She buzzed down her window, and in that moment, I knew that she was not only crazy, but loving the attention, lapping up the drama.

Yes, Pearl Robinson was a drama queen. She was trying to suppress a grin, which stretched across her full, wide lips.

I leaned into her open window. "Nutter. You want to get us both killed?" I couldn't help but smile too.

But, stubborn as ever, she continued her little game. "I meant what I said, Alexandre. I am not going to Vegas with you. I'm going to Kauai to see my dad."

"Oh Kauai now, is it? I don't think so." I opened her door and hovered my lips centimeters away from her face. "Correction. *We* are going to Vegas. *Together.*" I heard my own voice and I sounded so French… *togezzaire.* "We're getting married tonight; it's all arranged. Then we can go to Kauai for our honeymoon."

I *had* planned for Bora Bora, but who cared? As long as we sealed the deal, we could go anywhere. I grabbed the keys from the ignition and scooped Pearl into my arms and then flung her over my shoulder, so I had my hands free. She was kicking like a child, screaming like a little girl.

"Put me down Alexandre! This isn't funny!"

"Then why are you laughing?"

"Because this is preposterous! You're being outrageous!"

I strode over to the trunk of her car and took out her suitcase; a vintage Luis Vuitton, the weight of which was hard to manage with Pearl jiggling and kicking and flailing her arms about and thumping my back. My Taekwondo training certainly helped me manage this little vixen.

"Enough, Pearl. Stop behaving like a child. Or I'll have to spank you."

"Ha, very funny. You are *insane*, Alexandre Chevalier! Let me down! I won't marry you. I won't, I *won't!*"

"Yes, you will. Stop playing games."

"Don't you dare try and control me, you arrogant French shit!"

"Don't tell me what to do, Pearl. I know what I want and it's your crazy ass. You know it, and I know it. You *know* that we're meant to be together but you're just too stubborn to accept it right now. Stop wasting time because in the end, I'll get my way."

"Ha!" she squealed, still laughing. "You can't marry me because you don't have proof of my divorce!"

Pearl had underestimated me. I'd gotten my hands on her divorce papers weeks ago. "All taken care of, baby. All will be quite legal I can assure you."

I practically threw her into the back of my Mercedes and quickly locked the door. Child safety locks. She couldn't get out. She was pummeling the windows and I too, knew that I was behaving like a madman. But I didn't care. I wanted Pearl Robinson—soon to be Chevalier—and I wasn't going to take no for an answer. I drove off. I could see her through my rearview mirror pouting like a ten year-old in the back seat. The Sophie topic came up. Of course. Pearl was convinced, now, that Sophie was out to kill her.

She announced, "Laura called."

Shock horror! The word, 'Laura' made my body flush with heat and nausea. Had she revealed all to Pearl? *Oh, Jesus.* My stomach churned. *What is that psycho up to now?*

"She told me that Sophie is sure to have me killed in Vegas. That she owns chunks of it...hotels, everything; that she's powerful and owns politicians and police and—"

"Nonsense," I interrupted. I tried to sound nonchalant. It was true, Sophie did have important contacts in Vegas...did own hotels there. But the last thing she'd do was hurt Pearl. Hell, she wanted Pearl to be her friend! *Oh Laura, oh Laura, why can't you fucking stay out of my life?*

Pearl pounded her fist on the car seat. "Why are you ignoring me? Sophie will have me murdered—I'll end up in a dumpster somewhere in Vegas, all because you won't take this seriously!"

In that second, I so wanted to come clean. Tell Pearl about Laura drugging me. Assure her that Laura was making this rubbish up. But I knew that it would make things worse with Pearl. She was on the edge. Admitting that I'd had Laura on top of me, naked, would hardly be the right move—no, Pearl wouldn't have accepted that for a second. So I said nothing, just kept driving to Van Nuys airport where the jet would be waiting.

"Sophie's insane," Pearl went on. "She stabbed your father in the groin!"

Something in me snapped. If it hadn't been for Sophie, I'd be in a loony bin by now. I bashed my closed fist on the steering wheel. "Don't you fucking bring my monster father into this!" I shouted.

Pearl was silenced for a while. I could hear her uneven breathing. She really did believe that Sophie was going to have her topped off, but my hands were tied.

I changed gear. "She's jealous Pearl, that's all." What else could I say? *Laura tried to fuck me?* "Sophie will get used to you."

"She won't fucking get 'used' to me because I'm bailing, Alexandre. I value my life too highly. I love you. I'm *in* love with you, but I refuse to marry you with that crazy woman in the picture!"

The truth was on the tip of my tongue again. I wanted to blurt it all out. Assure her Laura was nuts. But if I did that, Pearl would want to know why. No, with the state she was in—her nightmares, her instability—now wasn't the time. So I just said, "I made some calls tonight. I'm selling HookedUp to Sophie, once and for all." It was only half a lie. I *had* discussed it with Sophie but nothing had been set in stone. "Satisfied?"

The truth was I wanted those wedding bands on our fingers, first. Seal the deal. My mission was to marry Pearl and sort the rest out afterwards. Typically male, I realized later. I should have laid all my cards on the table.

But I didn't.

And it got me into more of a mess than I imagined possible.

"Don't try and pussy-whip me, Pearl," I said, ridiculously grabbing onto any excuse, like a child holding onto a balloon, hoping it will whisk him up and away into some fantasy land.

There was silence and then Pearl said in a quiet voice, "I got pussy-whipped tonight."

Then the second set of secrets was revealed. Pearl told me that she found a photo of Sophie and Alessandra in an embrace.

So *that* was who Sophie was seeing. *Jesus, the plot thickened.* I looked guilty as Rex with a stolen bar of chocolate. The fact that I had no idea that Alessandra was Sophie's new romantic partner didn't let me off the hook. I hadn't told Pearl that Sophie was gay—that was her private life. Sophie was bailing out Samuel Myers and acting as a silent partner on *Stone Trooper.* Sophie and Alessandra were in each other's panties. Alessandra had also wheedled her way into Pearl's panties, or so it sounded from Pearl's pussy-whipped quip. *What a fucking tangle. All the more reason to abduct Pearl and take her away with me and get that bloody ring on her finger.*

"Interesting," I mused. "Sophie met Alessandra after that play we went to see her in in London." I laughed. This whole scenario could have been some silly sitcom.

"Did you hear what I said, Alexandre?" Pearl was leaning forward, still in the back seat, her angry breath on my neck. "I got pussy-whipped by Alessandra."

"Well I'm not surprised," I answered, coolly. "She was all over you."

"She seduced me and I let her! I have a sore ass. I'm a fucking head-case. Why the hell do you want to marry me, anyway? I'm a quasi lesbian. I can't do a work deal without being screwed. Yeah, I'm screwed in every way you look at it. I'm a mess, Alexandre."

I couldn't help but let a smile curve onto my lips. "I know."

"No you don't! You thought I was perfect!"

"Perfect for me, chérie. Perfect for me. I guess you must have figured out by now that I'm hardly normal myself. And what happened to you in the past has only made me love you more. We need each other, baby. We're both two dysfunctional peas in the same pod. And we won't be able to *dis*-function properly without one another, you'll see. If you try and run away from me, from *us*, you'll come back because we're destined to be together."

Famous last words.

Little did I know that 'run away' was exactly what Pearl had planned.

With the car parked, and Pearl desperate for the ladies room, we went inside the small airport of Van Nuys. She dashed to the toilets.

I waited for her. And waited.

I stood there like a fucking lemon, holding Pearl's handbag. At first I wasn't paying attention because I was so busy talking on my cell, organizing our wedding. What a fucking joke. I called the car rental people to ask them to come and pick up the car key from me. *Hang on a minute…where's the bloody key?* I fumbled in my jacket pocket…no key. *Did Pearl have it? No, why would she?* That was the first alarm bell. When I saw that the coast was clear and no other women were in the ladies room, I snuck in.

"Pearl? Hurry up, baby. Are you done?" She had told me that she needed to change her tampon. Nothing. The place was empty. I peered into all the cubicles. *What the fuck?* Then I saw…I looked up and there was a tiny window, wide open. I dashed out of the room, through some double doors, and onto the tarmac to the spot where I'd parked the Mercedes.

Gone.

She'd done a bloody runner! I looked in her bag and she had even left her phone behind. And her credit cards. She was *that* desperate to escape from me. A woman on the run. As if I were a wife-beater or something—she wanted nothing more than to get the hell away from me. Tears prickled my eyes. *This woman does not want me.* I felt as if a hole had been scooped out of my gut. Now I knew the British expression of 'feeling gutted.'

The jet was waiting.

But without Pearl, I had nowhere to go.

6

That whole night was torturous. I feared that in Pearl's state she'd drive off a cliff or something, so I called the car rental company and, as I suspected, they had a GPS system fitted underneath the car—Pearl could be tracked. I offered them a bribe, or as I liked to phrase it, "a big tip" so that I could keep her under my radar without causing too much fuss. But it was proving to be tricky because I hadn't included Pearl in the insurance policy (how the fuck was I to know that she'd make off with the car?) so I bought the car, instead. It was heading toward San Francisco. Good. She was on her way to her brother's, obviously. My head was like a computer unscrambling data. I couldn't find a solution to my predicament. The only words I heard ricocheting in my brain were, *Pearl doesn't want you Alexandre. Accept it.*

I made up my mind, then and there; I wasn't going to chase after her anymore. I'd take my own tried and tested advice: let her come to me—the bulldozer technique hadn't worked. I remembered a couple of adages—ironically given to me by my father (when he was in one of his kind moods): *What's yours won't go against you*, and *What's yours will come back to you*. Was Pearl mine? *I certainly felt she was.* I'd have to wait and see. Wait and see if she would return to me—be mine. And not only come back to me, but stick with me for good. I had to bide my time.

Having paid for the jet, I thought I might as well use it, so I flew straight to San Francisco and checked into a hotel. I totaled up the amount of hours it would have taken her to drive here, and I called Anthony, knowing that by now, she would have arrived. He denied that she was with him. More proof that she wanted out. I told him I had a team of detectives on the case. I wanted her to feel the gravity of what she'd done. I didn't need a detective; I myself was enough of a Sherlock Holmes to make up for the whole of Scotland Yard. But he believed me, I guess.

After I hung up, I listened to the messages on Pearl's phone. Most of them from me—but then one from Laura. I pressed my ear to the receiver and heard her sickly sweet-butter-wouldn't-melt-in-my-mouth tone:

"Pearl, you don't know me. I'm sorry to bother you like this. I finally tracked down your number. My name's Laura, Alexandre's ex…maybe you know who I am?"

I shook my head in disbelief. This woman was one hell of a piece of work.

"I'm calling to warn you. Sophie's really crazy. She could be out to hurt you. I'm sorry but…" at this point Laura did a nice little acting job; she sniffled down the line and put on a weak, pathetic, poor-me voice. "I had a terrible accident several years ago and could have died." *Wish you bloody had.*

The message rambled on in a Good Samaritan voice, ending with, "As one woman to another I thought I owed you this..."

I heard a guttural roar tear from my throat as I threw the cellphone against the wall and it smashed to the floor.

I was in this Laura shit up to my neck. She was such a good liar that I feared Pearl wouldn't believe me if I told her the real story. So I did what all guilty fools do; I dug myself in even deeper. I created more lies to cover myself. To this day, I will never forgive myself for this: I *lied* to Pearl.

The following afternoon, I waited for Pearl in Anthony's back yard. She came into the garden, her hair wet; she'd obviously been for a swim. She looked so beautiful in a bedraggled sort of way, her blonde hair loose over her shoulders, her eye make-up smudged. She looked as tired as I felt. I took her by surprise, as if she hadn't expected me. What did she think? That I wouldn't find her? I wanted to hug her there and then, take her in my arms, but my voice of reason kicked in and told me that I needed to stick to my plan. *Make her come to me. Don't suffocate her. Give her time to sort out her fucked-up state of mind.*

She stuttered, "Alexandre, I...I'm...I'm sorry, I didn't know what I was doing last night."

My lips tipped into a crooked, ironic smile and I took a step back. My pride kicked in. "Oh yes, you did, Pearl. You seemed to know exactly what you were doing."

"I...I...no, I had no choice—"

"I was standing there with a fucking lady's handbag while you climbed out of a bloody toilet window!" In that second, I almost wanted to laugh, call a truce; the whole drama was risible, but I stayed proud, immovable; I needed to drum it home to her how much she had hurt and belittled me. I gazed into her innocent blue eyes. Those eyes that had ripped my heart out. "Did that mean nothing to you? The fact that I wanted to marry you?" I could read the panic on her face.

She lifted up her arms and let them fall in an exasperated thump either side of her hips. "I still want to marry you, I still—"

"Don't you get it, Pearl? It's too late for that now," I lied.

She scraped her fingers through her wet hair and then covered her mouth with her hand. It was sinking in: the idea that she could lose me forever. Her pain was palpable. *Good. It shows that she still loves me.* But she was teetering on the edge—the edge of indecision. She could have gone either way. Rejection was quivering on her lips—she still wasn't ready to commit to me a hundred percent, and was using Sophie as an excuse. I needed all of her, every last percent. She was still obsessing about my sister, and if I admitted that I knew what Laura had done and that I'd listened to her voicemail, then I would have had to reveal the whole story of what had happened in London. This wasn't the time.

Sometimes in life you make dumb choices. And in that moment, everything I said, everything I did, was unforgivable.

So when Pearl brought up the subject of Laura's phone call, I pretended that she must have misinterpreted what Laura said. Because if Pearl knew what Laura's motives were—that Laura still wanted me—it might make her run from me for good. I couldn't risk that. Panicking, I told her that I'd lost her handbag with her phone and credit cards inside. That I'd reported it stolen. The fact that either of us could have listened to Laura's messages without the phone itself, didn't seem to register with Pearl. Perhaps she was in too much shock.

If I could do things over again, I would not have said what I said. But I did.

Coldhearted.

Bastard.

These were the words to describe me in that instant. Did I subconsciously want Pearl to suffer? Live the agony that I had undergone the night before? Know the stab of abandonment? Feel the desolation of knowing you have lost your other half? Perhaps I did. Because the more I spoke, the more immersed I became in my fabrication of the truth. Perhaps I thought that Pearl's pain was proof of her love for me. Knowing that she gave a shit about me gave me hope for our future.

The words that came out of my mouth showed that I wasn't going to let her off easily. No, she'd need to *earn* me back.

"You know what, Pearl? I'm done," I said, my eyes sharpened flints. "What you did to me last night pushed me to my fucking limit. You demonstrated, loud and clear, that you don't want me and that you're using Sophie as an excuse to run from me."

Pearl's mouth was an O. Her blue eyes round with disbelief. She stood there, shaking, her lips trembling. "I love you, Alexandre. Please, please let's work this out."

"Work what out?" And here, I really *did* mean what I said. I was fed up with this Sophie nonsense—Pearl thinking that Sophie was capable of murder, not believing that she wanted to make amends. She hated Sophie's guts long before the Laura message, and Sophie really had been trying. I went on, "Work what out, Pearl? As long as Sophie's breathing you won't let up. I can't have a relationship with someone who hates my sister, especially when she and I are in business together."

My monologue continued, as I explained to Pearl why Sophie was not her enemy, and culminating with a balm for her wound, I said, "Come here, chérie, and give me one last kiss before saying goodbye." It was if an actor were speaking, not me, and I, the onlooker, from the wings—the audience watching the performance. I was observing a coldblooded, callous bastard who was calculating every move—treating Pearl like an acquisition, not a human being. I knew what I was doing. I was a billionaire businessman and I always got what I wanted. And I wanted Pearl...

To be unequivocally mine.

This was my way of going about it.

"You're breaking *up* with me?" she whimpered.

"No, Pearl. It was *your* choice. You broke us up last night. You broke my heart in two."

"That's not what I want...*at all!*"

I continued my performance. "Say what you like, baby, but actions speak louder than words. Nobody should have to go what I went through. You discarded me like a piece of trash, leaving a waiting jet and a waiting fiancé while you climbed out of a fucking toilet window, like a six year-old playing hide-and-seek. Not to mention the reverend in Vegas, and the surprise I had planned for us after our wedding."

Her eyes lit up. "What surprise?" Ha! I'd piqued her interest. Good.

"It's the past now, baby. Water under the bridge." I leaned down and kissed her. A passionate, sexual kiss with my hand gripping her ass—to let her know what she'd be missing. I drew her against my thumping heart, and opened her lips teasingly with my tongue, probing, lingering—my cock coming alive with every stroke of my tongue on hers. (I'd piqued her interest—she'd 'peaked' mine.) She yielded to me and then, after I knew I had her attention, I pulled back. If she'd been smart, she would have known my speech was bullshit and that no man can kiss a woman like that when he's not head over heels in love. Not to mention the rock in my jeans.

"Give me another chance," she creaked out, tears spilling from her eyes.

I drew her closer and whispered in her ear, "No." Then I gave her another speech about all the gifts she'd be getting from me: the Mercedes, an apartment in Cap d'Antibes, the Porsche, a new apartment that I'd be renting for her, and HookedUp Enterprises itself. The list went on. Academic, because I knew we'd be sharing all these things in the future anyway. I had no doubt in my mind that she would be my wife. I wasn't going to give up on her—of course not—but she needed to pine for me. Needed to feel what life was going to be without me for a while.

My last words were, "Bye Pearl, baby. Look after yourself." I walked away, not looking behind.

Fuck I was being a bastard.

But it was the only way to win her back for good.

7

Money and power were my obsessions for many years, working around the clock to make HookedUp what it quickly became.

Now I had an obsession of a different nature: Pearl.

Every minute of every day, I wanted to be with her. Hold her. Make love to her, although she still probably wasn't ready for that, after all those nightmares about the college rapists. All the more reason for me to give her time to heal herself, to step away from her; for her to spend a while with her brother and father. She told me she was going to Hawaii to visit her dad.

Pearl and I were talking, but barely. My calls were clipped and businesslike. I sent her a Birkin handbag, replete with cellphone and replacements for her other 'stolen' stuff. She needed a new purse, anyway. The old one I stashed away in a suitcase.

Meanwhile, I waited, like a lonely crocodile in his patch of territory; no mate, no friends (except for faithful Rex), biding my time until Pearl wouldn't be able to bear being away from me anymore. Only then would I make my move.

I had two things to sort out: sell my share of HookedUp to Sophie, once and for all, and deal with the dreaded Laura.

If I wanted to make things work with Pearl, even if she were being irrational about Sophie, I had to extricate myself from HookedUp. Because, seriously, how much money and power does a person need? I'd proved myself—I'd never have to work again if I didn't want to. It was a small sacrifice to pay for a smooth road ahead with the woman I loved.

But Laura...*Jesus,* that was an unquantifiable problem waiting—like a grenade—to detonate.

I dialed her house number. I was hoping to get James on the line, to tell him what was going on—to get his crazy wife under control and keep her away from me for good. But James hadn't been answering his cell so I wasn't surprised when Laura picked up. As I stood in the kitchen in my apartment, I opened the fridge door, wondering what I should snack on, but the moment I heard Laura's voice, I lost my appetite.

"Hello darling" she cooed.

"How did you know it was me?" I asked with suspicion—I'd hidden my number.

"Gut feeling."

I slammed the fridge door shut so hard I heard a bottle smash. "I am not your darling, Laura. I don't ever, ever want to see you again. Your shenanigans with me at The Connaught were bad enough, but what you did to Pearl was beyond imagination. She was terrified. Terrified."

She chuckled. "That was the idea."

"I'm marrying Pearl so you might as well accept it and get out of my fucking life."

"You won't marry Pearl, Alex my love, when I tell you what I know."

Blood pounded in my ears. "What do you know?"

"I think it's something we need to discuss face to face. I'll come to New York—we can have a little chat."

"No!" And then I said calmly, "I have business to attend to in London. I'm going to Provence to see about house stuff—I'll pick up those books of yours and bring them over to your place. And I'll pick up my Aston Martin from your garage, too. That way, you and I will break all ties and we won't ever have to see each other again."

"So final. So dramatic! Well, Alex darling, if you like a little drama, I can guarantee you that I won't disappoint."

"No more games, Laura—really, this isn't funny."

"I thought our time together at The Connaught was hilarious, and if I remember rightly, you did too."

"The drugs had me laughing, but I can tell you it wasn't bloody funny standing with my dick poking out like a fucking torpedo in front of my sister and Indira Kapoor."

Laura cackled into the line, her breath hitching in hysterics.

"So when I next come to London, I'll bring those books, get my car and sayonara, okay?"

"No, Alex, it's not okay. I'm still in love with you. Surely you must have guessed that by now?"

"What you have for me, Laura, isn't love; it's some sort of sick obsession. If you loved me you'd want me to be happy. Please, I *beg* of you—leave me, and leave Pearl in peace to get on with our lives."

"But I can't do that—I want your baby."

I knew it! *That* was what she was after when she laced my Bloody Mary with Viagra, and God knows what else was in that cocktail. I hung up on her, my stomach coiling with fury. She was beyond insane. When she had her accident and the doctors said she hadn't suffered brain damage, I now knew they'd got the prognosis wrong. This woman was not right in the head. Okay, she had always been highly-strung, demanding and spoiled, but this? This behavior was psychotic.

My cell rang again. I ignored it. Laura, wanting to wind me up some more. But then I glanced at the screen and saw that it was Elodie. I opened the fridge again to get out a drink.

"Elodie," I said with relief, cracking open a beer, "what's up?"

"I'm outside your door. I forgot my key."

"The door's not locked, I'm in the kitchen." I gulped down the whole bottle of beer almost in one go and the fizz prickled my nose—Laura had made me thirsty.

Elodie giggled into the line. "Oh. Duh! Okay."

She came into the kitchen and I took a double take. She wasn't dressed in her usual Goth attire and she looked quite beautiful without all that black make-up on her eyes. She was wearing skinny jeans tucked into elegant, black boots and a pink, scoop-necked sweater which accentuated her delicate neck. But the headphones she was wearing still gave her a street-cool look. She was slim, as always, but didn't look like a scrawny sparrow anymore. I gave her a big bear-hug. I'd missed her. She hadn't been coming into the HookedUp offices much lately, because she said she was getting her art portfolio together.

"I was thinking about making an omelet or something. Are you hungry?" I asked.

She sat down. "What?"

"Take your headphones off and maybe you can hear me. What are you listening to, anyway?"

She took them off and disconnected her iPod. "She's a new singer from New Zealand, still in high school. This song, *Royals*, hasn't even been released yet, but a friend of mine got her hands on it—knows the producer or something."

"Hungry?"

"Sure."

I narrowed my eyes at her suspiciously. "Really, you're eating now?"

"A girl's got to eat."

"Great. That's great." I got some ingredients out of the fridge, cracked open some eggs and whipped them in a bowl. Elodie watched me with curiosity. I doubted she did any cooking herself. Lucky about the massive choice of take-out in New York or she probably would have starved from laziness.

"You're pretty flashy, breaking eggs with one hand."

"I worked as a sous chef in a restaurant in Paris once upon a time."

"I didn't know that," she said.

"There's a lot of stuff you don't know about me."

"I know that you and Maman left home very young and had to look after yourselves, but she never tells me details. What did she do as a job?"

"She worked as a waitress," I lied. "Hey, Elodie, I forgot to ask you; how's the portfolio coming along? Still taking photos? Still making those angry angel collages?"

"Going okay, I guess, but I need to get away for a while," she said, not wanting to look me in the eye.

I lit the gas. "What's wrong? You're not paranoid about being followed again, are you?"

"I need a break but I don't want to go back to Paris. I want to do some traveling or something. Backpack around Asia. I can go with my roommate, Claire."

"You know what? There's a lot to see right here in the United States. There's no need to go schlepping around dodgy foreign countries when there's too much unrest in the world right now. Go to the Grand Canyon or Yellowstone Park, why don't you?"

To my surprise, she replied, "Okay, good idea."

I tore some fresh basil leaves, sprinkling bits into the pan, and suddenly had a thought. "I have a car...well, it's Pearl's car. It's in San Francisco and needs to be brought to New York. Is your driver's license in order? And your friend's?"

Elodie got up and took a couple of beers out of the fridge and offered me one. "Yup. Cool plan. Can we take as long as we like to drive cross-country?"

"Sure. No rush. Just be careful. Don't go over the speed limit—be prudent. Speak to my assistant, Jim—he can get you your plane tickets there, hotels, whatever you need. Maybe you can even stay with Pearl's brother. Anyway, the car's at his place in his garage. I'll call Anthony and Pearl and get it all arranged. I'm sure Pearl won't mind—actually you'd be doing her a favor."

"Why is Pearl's car in San Francisco? I thought you guys had gone to LA?"

"We did, but she stayed on. Went to visit Anthony. Now she's in Hawaii visiting her dad."

Elodie ran her gaze over me, dissecting me, drilling her eyes into my thoughts. "You look guilty, Uncle Alexandre. What's going on with you and Pearl?"

"Nothing." I tried to suppress the heat-rush I felt, by turning on the sink faucet and putting the underside of my wrists under cold running water. A trick I learned in the Foreign Legion. As if on cue, my cell started buzzing. The words LAURA popped up on the screen. Elodie picked up my cell without pressing anything, but saw who the caller was.

She arched her brows. "Well aren't you going to answer it?"

I shook my head. *Fucking psycho Laura, leave me alone!*

"She called *me* the other day, you know. She wanted to know Pearl's number. What's up?"

"Keep away from Laura, Elodie. Don't answer her calls and do not, whatever you do, give her any information about *anything* or *anybody* at all."

"But Laura's nice! She was always really friendly to me."

"*Was* is the operative word. That accident changed her."

"So what's that got to do with Pearl? Why does Laura want to get in touch with her? Why didn't you go with Pearl to Hawaii?"

I switched off the gas burner. "Would you get us a couple of plates and utensils?"

Elodie got up. "Why didn't you go to Hawaii with her?" she asked again.

"She needed space. Needed to sort a few things out."

"I doubt it. Pearl's crazy about you—anyone can see that. It's *you*, I bet, playing games. Playing 'I need space' games. So typical."

"We both need a little break."

"Yeah, right. That's male code for "back off.""

"Not at all. I want to be with Pearl...she just needs some time on her own and—"

"Ha! You're just making excuses so that you can behave how you like without any thought for Pearl."

"You've got it all wrong, Elodie."

She sneered at me. "I don't know what you're doing, juggling two women at once. Typical man behavior. As if male babies were born with a mean gene in them. You're all the same—*all* of you. The only difference is, some hide it better than others but the bastard gene is buried into every man's DNA."

She had a point. "That, mademoiselle, is a very uncalled for and rude accusation!"

She put the plates on the table. "I know more about men than you think." She blew air out of her lips—pouting while she spoke.

"Elodie, I thought you were meant to be going to art college this fall anyway, not traveling about and wasting your time." I served up our omelets and sat down.

"Next year."

"Don't procrastinate."

She rolled her eyes. "Yeah, yeah, yeah."

"And cool it with the cocky attitude, okay?"

She gave me a salute. "Okay, sir!"

Elodie was right. I had the bastard gene in my DNA. What was I playing at? All this, *Let Pearl come to me,* was bullshit. I loved Pearl. Damn it, I couldn't be happy without her. I was going to go and find her, whether she was ready or not. I was so in love with Pearl Robinson, I couldn't concentrate on anything else.

We belonged together and I didn't want to spend one more day without her. I'd already wasted enough time.

I'd been tracing Pearl's movements with the tracking device I'd installed on her new cellphone. Guilty. Guilty of obsession, possessiveness, jealousy, and controlling, manipulating behavior of every kind. I convinced myself that all I was doing was keeping a distant eye on her, in case of any emergency; that I could be wherever she was like a knight in shining armor, ready to save her should the occasion rise. Except, my armor was a little rusty, the metal too bulky. Maybe when I was seven years old I'd been a good *chevalier,* a good knight, but now I'd lost the flair. She had been in London for several days. Why? Instead of catching a plane from Hawaii to New York, she'd gone there. Hampstead to be precise. I remember her having told me that Daisy's mother lived there.

By this point, I knew I needed to go and join her.

I stopped off at my house in Provence first. The pool was being fixed so I had a meeting with the builders, stayed the night, picked up those bloody books of Laura's, and left. Technically, a few of the books were mine; gifts from her. I could have taken them to Goodwill, or the French equivalent, but somehow getting them free and clear of my house and giving them back to Laura was symbolic—a fresh start for Pearl and me. Returning gifts to the gift bearer sends a clear, no-nonsense message—*get out of my life; not even your gifts hold any meaning anymore.*

I took a nice, small and discreet room, not at The Connaught, but another hotel, just in case Laura decided to track me down. Annoyingly, when I asked one of the members of staff to wrap some gifts for my mother—some cashmere scarfs I'd bought—they also giftwrapped the bloody box of books. I didn't have time to unwrap it. But the last thing I wanted was for Laura to believe I was showering her with gifts or there was some good, pre-Christmas feeling on my part. No, I wanted to ice her out. I'd go there, give her the books and get my Aston Martin, which James had been kindly looking after for me—it was parked in their garage which I still had the keys to. I'd asked him to run the engine every now and then to keep it tuned. I'd bought the car in England and had hoped to drive it to France with Pearl, but we hadn't had a chance. Right now, the idea of my precious classic car being anywhere near Laura was making me nervous—I could just imagine her dousing it with acid or something, stripping off the beautiful gunmetal-gray paintwork.

I couldn't wait to snip all ties with her.

8

The hotel didn't have a gym so I used one close by. I wanted to expend some of the pent-up, surplus energy I had, which was playing tricks with my brain; making me angry and quietly aggressive. I knew part of the reason was because I hadn't had sex for nearly two weeks. It shouldn't have affected me; I'd been without sex for long stretches before, when I was in the French Foreign Legion, but that was before I met Pearl. She was imprinted on my brain. I tossed and turned at night, smelling her, hearing her sweet voice, feeling that silky soft skin, dreaming of fucking her. Hearing her whimper when she came, the tears that would fall when her orgasm was so intense she couldn't believe it was true.

After the gym, I showered, then checked my cell to see Pearl's whereabouts. A rush of adrenaline spiked my veins; she was at James and Laura's house! What the fuck? Not only was Laura playing games with me, but she was obviously fucking with

Pearl, too. Regret washed over me—I should have warned Pearl—told her how dangerous Laura was. She must have called Pearl again after the 'Sophie is a killer call' to set up some sort of meeting. I dashed over to my hotel to grab the box of books and set off in the direction of Chelsea. Finally, I could deal with the problem in situ. I'd confront Laura with Pearl right there; Laura's lies would be etched across her face and Pearl would believe me. We could be rid of Laura, once and for all; face the music together as a couple. I hailed a cab and jumped in, giving the taxi driver Laura's exclusive Chelsea address.

I thought back to my code; treating women with respect at all times, no matter how unhinged they were. Bad idea. I should have told the lot of them to fuck off a long time ago. Laura, Claudine, even Indira. After the way my father treated my mother, I swore I'd always be gentle with women in every circumstance—the idea of being like him in any way disgusted me. But my kindness wasn't paying off; it had got me in a tangled web with a whole lot of Black Widow spiders out to gobble me up.

"Can you please step on it—don't mean to be rude but I'm in a hurry," I said to the driver who was chatting away in his Cockney accent about immigration.

"No problem, gov. It's those bastard eastern European scum and the like. Vey come 'ere expectin' work, stealin' jobs from decent British citizens. Arf of 'em 'av illegal, dodgy businesses, drugs, prostitution and ve like—vey really are ve scum of ve earf." *They really are the scum of the earth,* I finally realized he was saying.

"Is there a shortcut?" I suggested.

At first he thought I was engaging in conversation so I repeated, "Can we get there any faster? It's an emergency."

He swerved to the right and took a narrow street through the back of Belgravia. "Are you Rumanian, or sumfing?"

"No. French."

"Like a few frogs legs, do ya? Snails?" He laughed at his joke.

Finally we arrived. I shoved too many pound notes in the driver's hand, not waiting for change, and dashed to Laura and James's front steps, rapping hard on the brass doorknocker. Laura came out and grinned at me, flinging her arms about me as if we were two long-lost, passionate lovers. I held the box of books out and pushed my way through the door.

"How lovely, Alex—you brought me a present; how sweet of you."

Once inside the house, I shouted, "Pearl? Are you here?"

Laura started laughing. "She just left."

I dropped the box on the marble floor; it landed with a thud. "Damn! How long ago?"

"Ten minutes."

"Damn," I cursed again.

"She doesn't want to see you, Alex, so I wouldn't get your knickers in a twist."

I wanted to ignore her quip but heard myself ask, "She said that?"

"Yes. She came to England especially to see me."

"Bullshit Laura."

"It's not bullshit. She told me you'd split up and that she'd had enough and was going to start dating other men. That she'd had time to mull things over in Hawaii. She said she didn't have time for silly games and that she understood that you were too immature for her—she wants to go out with someone her own age."

I wanted to believe that Laura was lying but she knew about Pearl being in Hawaii—her conversation with Elodie had been before Pearl had even decided to go to Hawaii. Laura's words stung like little poison darts. Perhaps there was an element of truth to them. I *had* been acting immaturely and it wasn't a surprise Pearl wanted to date a more mature man. Fuck! I now regretted leaving her in tears in the backyard at her brother's. Begging me to give her another chance, I pretended her words were empty. I'd behaved like a total, coldblooded bastard. In that moment—in Anthony's garden—it hadn't occurred to me that Pearl had choices; she could simply dump me. Dump me at the drop of a hat. She was gorgeous—she could get any man. What the fuck had I been thinking?

I stood there, remembering how it was *Laura* that had intensified Pearl's fear of Sophie, with that crazy phone call getting us into this mess. My eyes were pools of ice as they locked with hers. "I've brought your books back, Laura. The hotel gift-wrapped the box by mistake so don't get any grand ideas. I'm leaving now, I'm going to get my car." I strode down the hall towards the garden, which led to the garage.

"Alex, wait!" Laura limped after me with her cane. "Why are you so pissed off? I thought we could have some tea and have a heart-to-heart."

"Yeah, right, Laura. I'm really going to drink your tea, laced with some bloody drug. You behaved like a fucking psycho last time we met and what you did to Pearl was unforgiveable. Un-fucking-forgivable. You should go and get professional help—I'd offer to pay for a shrink but I don't want to be involved with you in *any way, whatsoever.* Is the garage locked?"

"It's unlocked," she said sulkily, as if what I told her was a surprise. "You know where the buzzer is for the garage door and you still have your own keys, I suppose. Alex, don't be a spoil-sport—*come* on."

I suddenly thought of something. "You didn't give *Pearl* a cup of tea, did you?"

Laura smirked.

I grabbed her by the shoulders and found myself shaking her. I'd never hurt a woman in my life. *Jesus!* But the temptation to slap her was overwhelming. My heart was pounding, my breath unsteady. I stepped back, sucked in a calming lungful of air, let go of her, and said in a quiet voice, my teeth clenched, "Did you offer Pearl a cup of tea?" If I had been like Michael Corleone—as Pearl so often described me—I would have felt no qualms about having Laura eliminated. But I wasn't. I respected a person's life too much—God knows, I'd been responsible for enough deaths to see me well into the depths of Hell—I didn't want another on my conscience. And however crazy Laura had become, we had shared something once. You can't wipe away your past.

"Yes, I offered her tea," but she quickly added, "she didn't want any, though."

I exhaled a sigh of relief, marched off, swung open the back door and raced towards the garage. My beautiful 1964 DB5 Aston Martin was under a tarpaulin, and when I peeled it back, I was both surprised and delighted to see that it was unblemished. What a beauty! No wonder this model had starred in two Bond films. I got into the front seat, humming *Skyfall* to myself, and inhaled the wonderful aroma of Classic Car (*they really should learn to bottle this*). For a second or two, the wonder of my car soothed away the fury I felt with Laura. But then I turned the key. Dead. Bloody nothing. My blood rose again. The battery was fucking dead! I got out and saw Laura standing there, her lips quirked into another victorious smile. Had she done this on purpose?

"James is away so hasn't been here to start the engine. *Poor Alexandre*," she said, sarcasm dripping from her languid, snooty tongue. "Anyway, the delay will be perfect—I'll change into something more comfortable while you recharge the battery, then while we wait for it to juice-up, we can have a heart-to-heart."

"No, Laura. I'm off. *Now*. Suresh can come and pick up the car at some point; I don't have time for this nonsense and the last thing I want right now is a cozy chat with you." I slammed the car door shut, sheathed my pride and joy with its cover, then stormed over to the red button on the wall, which I pressed with vigor. The garage door buzzed open. I shot out under the narrow space, as Laura shouted after me, but I legged the hell out of there.

I didn't want to see Laura's brazen face ever again.

9

I called Pearl but her cell was off. I wanted to explain the whole Laura fiasco, minus the Bloody Mary incident. I still couldn't bring myself to admit that it ever happened. I felt ashamed of myself being trussed up, hands bound, body numb—as immovable as a Christmas turkey about to be delved into. It made me feel like a real fucking fool. One day I'd tell Pearl—after I'd gotten a ring on her finger, but right now wasn't the time.

I wondered how much longer she'd be staying in London. I debated whether I should go to Hampstead—to Daisy's mother's house—and just wait outside the front door for Pearl until she came back. Then my cell went. I hoped it was her calling me but then it hit home, *Why on Earth would Pearl call me now? She's given up on me. Not interested. Can't be bothered with my stupid games and I don't blame her.*

I pressed 'talk'. It was Sebastian, my new video game partner. "What's up?" I asked.

"Do you have time for a pint?" I'd forgotten that—the British are always talking about 'pints down the pub.' I weighed my options. I really did want to just get going to Hampstead. Be that stalker.

"No," I answered in a flat voice. "You've caught me at a bad time."

"I really need you to meet our other programmer. Just for five minutes. You know, you can always tell in the first few seconds if you like a person or not. I'd rather you checked him out, personally."

"I trust your judgment, Sebastian."

"He's coming over to the office so I thought we'd pop round the pub just to make him feel at ease."

"The one around the corner from the office?"

"Yeah, The Lamb and Flag."

I looked at my watch. Covent Garden was pretty much *en route* to Hampstead. "Okay but just five minutes."

I hailed a cab.

After our brief pub meeting—the new guy nervous but a good, hard-working type and apparently very talented—I stood outside the pub on the street, amidst the traffic, and tried calling Pearl again. I'd noticed that London had become a fascinating melting pot of foreign bodies, fluttering and weaving about like ribbons of different colored flags through the busy streets. Nobody spoke English here anymore; Brazilians, French, Italians, Germans, South Americans, all having made London their home—was anyone British? (Except the taxi drivers—the opposite of New York City.) The phone rang and rang. No bloody answer. My cell buzzed in my hand—it made me jump. It was Sophie.

"Why didn't you tell me you were in London, Alexandre? I'm here, too. We could have met up."

"What for?" My voice was clipped. Sophie was not my favorite person in the world right now. In fact, *everyone* was getting under my skin since Pearl and I had been parted for the last two weeks. I'd been edgy, snappy and volatile. "How did you know I was in London?"

"That's why I'm calling. Pearl told me. We bumped into each other. She just dropped me off in Hampstead."

"She dropped *you* off? She rented a car?"

"No. She's with my driver. I dropped in to see a friend up here. Pearl and I crossed paths in Harrods. What a coincidence, eh? She confirmed what you told me about Laura's lies. Said she'd been at Laura's and recounted the whole freaky story—that Laura said I'd tried to kill her—that her accident was my fault. Fucking crazy! Alexandre, I don't know what game you're playing seeing Laura still, but Pearl loves you. *Really* loves you. She told me she saw you at Laura's house. Entering her front door. What the hell were you doing there? Are you *fucking* her?"

"Of course not. I was taking those bloody English books back and went to get my car."

"Well you should stay away from that little bitch—she has it in for you."

"Yeah, I'm coming to that very same conclusion. She's insane. Did Laura mention the Bloody Mary fiasco to Pearl?"

"I don't think so—if she did, Pearl didn't mention it. Pearl told me you'd split up, that you didn't want to give her the time of day and that you were dating Laura again. You're not lying to me, are you? It's not true, is it?"

"What do you think? Of course bloody not."

"I didn't think so. We bonded, Alexandre. For the first time ever, Pearl was open with me. She was crying and everything—she's so distraught and brokenhearted. I felt so guilty for having been such a bitch to her. Poor thing, she's really hurting right now. She's so in love with you, Alexandre. So in love."

I felt an ache in my solar plexus. *Poor Pearl. She must be confused out of her mind.* "Well I'm going to hail a cab right now and go up to Hampstead."

"She won't be there now. She just zipped by the house to get her suitcase and say goodbye to Daisy's mother—I told my driver to take her to Heathrow Airport."

"Where's she going?"

"To New York."

"Do you know what time?"

"I do, actually. She'll be leaving about ten thirty. She's flying with American Airlines." All Sophie's information was computing in my brain. There was no point going to Hampstead now. I'd get on a plane myself to New York—get there first and wait for Pearl at her new apartment—the one I'd rented for her. Ha! I even had a spare set of keys. She wouldn't be able to avoid me.

I called the airline and got her upgraded to First class with special instructions to take extra care of her. That was the least I could do.

Thanks to the private jet company I use (yes, I'm really green, really ecological with my great, big, black, carbon footprint), I got back to New York ahead of Pearl and in time to organize a few things.

I had several boxes of groceries delivered, with everything essential for a new apartment, and stocked up the fridge with food. The place was perfect for Pearl; two bedrooms, a smart marble bathroom. Pre-war but sleekly furnished in neutral colors, and with all the mod cons. However, I was now kicking myself. I wanted her to come back home where she belonged: to *my* apartment.

I waited patiently, making a few business calls in between checking her whereabouts. She had arrived at JFK. A driver would be there to collect her but with strict instructions not to let her know that I was the one who sent him—*let her believe it's Sophie.*

I wanted to take her by surprise when she came home. Make it so she couldn't say no.

An hour or two later, I heard the key turn in the lock and I quickly opened the door. Pearl fell into me, landing in my waiting arms, surprised as hell, obviously mistaking me for a rapist or a burglar—and I thought for a second, *That's me, the burglar who wants to rob her independence, steal her for myself.* And a rapist, because all I had been thinking about was fucking her, despite my conscience telling me it was wrong, that she wouldn't be ready, that if I'd been a 'good' person, sex would have been the last thing on my mind.

"Pearl, baby. I've missed you so much. I'm so in love with you—I can't live without you. I've been climbing the walls." My feelings spilled out of my mouth in a torrent. I could feel my nose burning as my eyes misted up. She looked so beautiful; her blonde hair mussed up, her cheeks glowing from the cold night. I gathered her tightly in my arms, bringing her close to my chest and kissing the top of her head to hide my face. I didn't want her to see my wet eyes. Her hair smelled so sweet—I breathed her in. My savior, my life.

"Get off me!" she screamed as she struggled from beneath my amorous grip. "What kind of game are you playing Alexandre Chevalier? You're with Laura now!"

"No, baby. No! I love *you.*"

"Why are you torturing me? Leave me alone."

I couldn't help myself. I started to kiss her ravenously, licking her lips, forcing my way in; anything to quell her suspicions, to wipe Laura from her mind. My cock was rock-hard against her belly, pounding in my pants. I loved Pearl but my insatiable need for her after being apart for so long was overwhelming. "Please baby, believe me, I am so *not* with Laura."

"Don't lie! I saw you entering her front door! I saw you with my own eyes!" Pearl pushed me away, rapping her fists against my chest.

I quietly closed the front door. Her suitcase was still outside but I feared the whole building would be woken with the noise. For the next few minutes the banter continued; Pearl's accusations and my defense. Yet I could hardly concentrate on the conversation: my eyes hooded with longing, my groin raging. All I wanted was for us to fuck and forget this Laura nonsense, but I had to calm Pearl down first. I could see it in her eyes too—she wanted me urgently but her head was telling her to protect her heart. Yet right now, her heart was telling her to make love to me. I could read it in her gaze, her tweaked nipples. She was hungry for me. Fucking ravenous.

I stepped close to her again and took her flailing wrists. "Pearl, my darling—please, please let's just be close. I've missed you like crazy."

"Bullshit! You haven't even called me!"

"I did call you. Today actually, but your cell was switched off."

"Big deal! *Finally,* after all this time making me suffer, making me plan my life without you, you call. You call when you feel like a fuck! You want to be with Laura but you're using me. For sex. Laura was right, you're only in 'lust' with me—all your marriage talk was bullshit."

Yeah, a waiting jet and a huge rock of a ring is bullshit. I realized this Laura thing had taken over her mind. Not letting her see coherently. "NO! Pearl, I *do* want to marry you."

"Oh, so you can have little wifey waiting for you at home while you go off and have affairs! I'm not that kind of girl, Alexandre. Maybe there are plenty of women out there who would stand that kind of marriage for the luxuries you can provide, with all your money, but I don't *care* how rich you are! I just want a faithful husband; a man who sees *only* me." Her eyes flashed like warning lights, the blue a deep, glimmering ultramarine.

I kissed her hand. I dared not do more—her wrath was impressive; her fire blazing. "I only see *you,* Pearl, I swear. It's been hell for me. I've missed you like crazy—I've been obsessing about you night and day. I've been going around with a hard-on for two weeks—please calm me down, chérie—I feel like an animal. I need you. I need you baby." Bad little speech that one. It made her rage all the more—it sounded as if I only wanted her for sex. The whole 'books in the box' saga was dredged up. More explanations while Pearl raised her eyebrows at me with suspicion and disdain. I explained the gift-wrapped box, the fact that I'd gone to Provence, first, and why I hadn't sent it by mail. I finally thought I'd won her over. But no.

Not even close.

"That doesn't explain how Laura knew so much about me. She said you'd called me a "loony with a slutty past." Pearl pushed me away again and tossed her head in disgust. "You told Laura my secrets, things about my private life. About Alessandra, because Laura just happened to know *everything!*"

I had been able to explain my movements and reasons up until now, but not this. How *did* Laura have all that information? Sophie hadn't spoken to her, and Elodie didn't know that stuff. I thought back. Had Elodie listened in on one of my private conversations with Pearl? No. *How the fuck did Laura know all this?* The argument between Pearl and me went on, back and forth. Pearl not believing me. A bolt of rage shot through me.

I shouted, "I don't fucking *know* how Laura knew that stuff but I *love* you, I want to marry you and I don't want Laura fucking well *near* me! You *have* to believe me!" I roared so loudly that the sound echoed through the fresh, newly decorated apartment.

Finally Pearl was silent. The drama had appeased her. I saw her breathing was erratic, her lips parted and her gaze flicked down to my crotch and then to my eyes. *Her look said, Please just fuck me—I can't take this mistrust.* Make-up sex. I couldn't wait a second more. I had to get my tailored pants off—my dick was wedged uncomfortably beneath the fine wool fabric like a massive steel rod. I closed in on Pearl, pinioning her wrists above her head with one hand as I slowly unzipped her jeans with the other. She let me, as she nipped her bottom lip between her teeth and moaned quietly. I eased my hand inside her panties and felt her oozing moisture trapped there, waiting to explode.

I growled into her mouth as I kissed her, my fingers entering her liquid warmth, "That's it, no more drama games Pearl—you want this as much as I do."

I gathered her in my arms, carried her into the bedroom and threw her on the bed. Being a gentleman was not the first thing on my mind in that moment. The scene that ensued was hectic, wild, both of us like savage beasts. We ripped off our respective clothing, both acting like a pair of jungle cats in heat. Pearl spread herself out like a starfish—wanton—on the bed. I lay on top of her, no time to lose. But ever the little actress, she then squeezed her thighs together, trying not to let me enter her, meanwhile kissing me frantically, her slick pool beckoning me to stretch her wide open. She wanted me to ravage her. Play the dominant.

"Don't pretend you don't want this," I said, my hips pumping into her as I fucked her dripping wet clit. "You want me to despoil your tight little pussy?" The crown of my cock was going to detonate any second. I kept the rhythm up, sliding my length up and down her slit, the pressure of her tight, worked-out thighs like vices around my dick, not letting me in. This game was really arousing me—Pearl's thighs squeezing the sides of my cock as she whimpered and moaned beneath me.

"Oh baby, fucking you is like flying on a cloud straight to

Heaven." I grabbed the mane of her hair as I fucked that nub relentlessly until she couldn't hold out any longer—she opened her thighs and I slipped right in. Deep. Cramming her full. *Oh fuck!*

"This wet, hot pussy can't deny me, baby. Whatever your brain tells it to do, it has a mind of its own." I slammed into her hard and she cried out. I made little circular movements, my hips grinding round and round as I found her G-spot—her already sensitized clit was swollen like a ripe fruit.

She opened her thighs even further, maneuvering her body and hooking her ankles around my neck, bucking her hips up at me, as she clawed her nails into my ass and started shuddering beneath me. Usually she screamed, but this time she started weeping. "I'm coming, baby," she whimpered through tears, "I'm coming so hard."

My button was pressed. My thick cock expanded even more as I felt her pussy contract around me, sucking me in, gobbling me up with its avaricious grasp. I thrust back and forth merciless-ly and she started screaming, as I exploded inside her, my scorching seed shooting into her womb. I sucked her neck like a vampire needing blood. I had to have her taste on my tongue; I needed to mark her. As I pumped my orgasm into her, she climaxed again. I accentuated my thrusts with each word. "I. Love. Fucking. You. My cock thinks about you. All. Day. Long. All. Fucking. Day. Long. Your. Wet. Pearlette. Always. Ready to be fucked by my….Big. Hard. Horny. Cock." More of my cum spurted inside her as I moved my mouth from her neck to her lips and lashed my tongue on hers, sucking, licking, locking together. The rampant carnal fireworks between us were insane.

"Are you cured of your cock phobia?" I asked, knowing the answer as she moaned into my mouth.

"Oh yeah, oh God Alexandre, as long as it's you. I'm still coming, baby...*oh my God!*"

There was no way we could stay apart anymore. We were addicted to each other. We had to fuck like this every day. We had to satiate each other's craving for one another.

For the next twelve hours it was intermittent sparring, followed by make-up sex. Then Pearl would get suspicious again; the cross-questioning *Homeland*-style would begin once more, with me trying to explain. Then I'd fuck her again, and so on. Was it the drama that turned us on so much? Pearl getting me wild and emotional with her cool games which got me simmering with pent-up irritation and desire? It seemed she loved playing cat and mouse so that I would then ravage her, dominate her; fuck the coolness out of her—make her crumble beneath me. Sexually, she was a natural submissive and this was bringing out my bestial instincts. It worried me and excited me. I didn't want to fight; I wanted a smooth ride but I asked myself if the kind of ride Pearl desired was more of a roller coaster. Or perhaps she was just testing me to see if I was worthy of her love.

But I couldn't blame her suspicion about Laura. The question still remained unanswered. How the fuck *did* Laura know all those intimate things about Pearl? I sure as hell hadn't let anything slip. Had someone betrayed me?

10

Pearl's resolve to keep me on my toes continued for the next couple of weeks. The chill of the winter air seemed to match her emotions. She refused to move back in with me. Daisy and Amy took up residence with her in her new apartment, which meant I didn't have her all to myself. Daisy had split with her husband who had cheated on her—all the more reason why Daisy was acting like a guardian phoenix—always on the lookout, scrutinizing me with quiet reserve to see if I behaved well; if I did right by Pearl. Yes, I was on probation; all female eyes monitoring my every move, even little Amy who was only five years old.

Pearl had been trying to get in touch with Laura. She wanted a direct explanation from her. How, she wanted to know, did she have all that personal information? I sure as hell wanted to know too, and at that point—considering my line of work and now knowing how scheming Laura was—I stupidly hadn't put two and two together. What a dunce.

As for Pearl, she just didn't trust me—about Laura, about the history of my father—no she didn't buy my tale that he'd just 'disappeared into thin air,' and would slip it into the conversation every so often. I so wanted to reveal my secret, be honest with her, but it wasn't my call. I was protecting someone who had sworn me to secrecy.

I wanted to be as close to Pearl as possible but I felt that she was only half mine. We were still having sex, but somehow the situation was very confusing to me. She had discovered a new-found joy: sex without full-on commitment. It was as if she were twenty-two again. All those wasted years in her twenties and thirties after the rape—some of those married years (when she had been emotionally and sexually blocked), were given a new lease on life—her inner 1960's-sexual-revolution-babe had been unleashed. She'd become like a young Jane Fonda. I could hardly complain, but I was wondering if our marriage would *ever* go ahead. Pearl had what she wanted: me at her beck and call, 'servicing' her, filling her up' but without binding herself to me. She even had a nickname for me: the Exxon Guy. I laughed at her joke—what else could I do?

Talk about an odd juxtaposition of roles; it was as if she were my age and *I* was forty. All I could think of was getting rings on our fingers, while she stalled me with excuses. The bottom line was her wavering mistrust.

And just as I thought that there was a beam of light at the end of this tunnel (yes, the word tunnel could sound crass), an earthquake separated us as if we had been standing on the San Andreas fault line itself—Pearl and I seemed doomed. Just when

I thought that I, the frog, had a chance of becoming Pearl's prince by finally getting that magical, proverbial kiss, Laura chucked parts of me into her bubbling cauldron, stirring me in with her poisonous ingredients.

Eye of newt, and toe of frog,
Wool of bat, and tongue of dog.
Adder's fork, and blind-worm's sting,
Lizard's leg, and owlet's wing,
For a charm of powerful trouble,
Like a hellbroth boil and bubble.
Double, double toil and trouble,
Fire burn and cauldron bubble.

Shakespeare's lines—which I'd once learned at school—reverberated in my brain. I was busy shopping at Dean & DeLuca when Laura caught me by surprise. I had been eyeing up delicious Stilton cheeses and Christmas cakes and cookies but now I felt like throwing up.

"Darling," Laura purred into the line like the *Macbeth* witch she was, "so glad we're going to finally get a chance to chat."

My mouth was a thin hard line, my teeth clenched like clamps. "I have nothing to say to you, Laura, I'm going to hang up."

She quickly replied, "If you don't want your mother to be arrested for murder, you'd better hear me out."

I felt like a cartoon character being steamrolled. I looked down at my feet and saw that I was still in one piece but my body was experiencing a strange flattening sensation as if I were actually part of the floor itself.

I did a fake, raucous laugh. "You have a great imagination, Laura."

"Alex, I'm not in the mood to play your beating around the bush game. I've given you so many chances to make amends with me—nothing has worked so now I'm going to have to get tough."

"I don't have time for this nonsense, I'm hanging up." But I didn't hang up. I couldn't. I stayed on the line, my brain desperately trying to find a way out. I cast my gaze furtively around the store to see if eyes were on me but people were too busy shopping for holiday treats to notice. I said nothing more, just waited to see what would come next.

She went on, "I mean it. I have evidence. You were a fool to leave hip replacement parts hidden in that bookshelf. You supposed, I'm sure, that nobody would have known what they were. Well I *did.*"

Jesus! It had simply slipped my mind! "I got those bits of junk from a *vide grenier,*" I said with a weak chuckle, knowing she wouldn't buy my lie. As if I would buy hip replacement parts at a yard sale.

"Traceable, Alex, and you know it. Because if the patient has trouble after an operation—years later—the prosthesis needs to be traced to the manufacturer. Same thing with the teeth that I found stuffed inside a chopped out encyclopedia. Dental records, Alex. And just like the hip parts, I'd say those teeth belonged to a man. A man that I would also say, quite definitely, was your own father."

"You're insane, Laura," I croaked out, my mouth dry as desert sand.

"Scotland Yard might not think I'm so insane. We all watch CSI. Things are very state-of-the-art these days with forensics."

"I have no idea what you're talking about."

"I have proof. Has your mobile phone been acting up a little lately?"

Duh. How had I been so dumb? In my line of work, especially! She'd bloody listened in on my calls or seen a text message. I knew that it was possible these days. Without even touching someone's cell you could eavesdrop on a conversation. Calls, text messages—everything could be monitored by the intruder, even if you weren't actively talking on the phone. Spyware had become so advanced the cell could act as a recording device—as if the listener were sitting right next to you. I thought of a call I'd made to my mother back in the summer, telling her...what *had* I told her? I couldn't even remember but whatever it was, Laura had cottoned on. She'd been eavesdropping on Pearl, too. That's how Laura knew all those intimate details about her shenanigans with Alessandra. *What a dunce I'd been not to preempt that!*

"Alex? Are you still there?'

"Yes, I'm still here." I couldn't do any more denying. "What do you want, Laura? Money?"

"Don't be silly! What I want money can't buy."

"Most things have a price. What's your price, Laura?"

"Happiness."

"You *have* happiness: a very kind husband, a stunning house, money. Your health is back. What *more* do you want?"

"Simple. I want you."

"You know that's impossible."

"Your choice. Either your mum ends up rotting in jail or you be nice to me."

If only Pearl hadn't done a runner! We'd be married. A wife can't be forced to testify against her husband. We'd be a team. I stood there in silence in the middle of the store, amidst the beautiful display of gourmet foods. I was speechless. My fist was clenched in a ball while the other hand clawed the receiver of my cell. I had to sort this shit out. Now. I had visions in my head of a bus mowing Laura down, or her choking to death on a fish bone.

I heaved out a long breath and said, "I'll come and see you in London and we can talk this through."

"Good boy. I knew you'd see the light. I'll expect you by latest tomorrow. No stalling, Alex. Can't wait to see you, darling. Bye, bye."

I bought an apple juice, glugged it all down in one go and called my mother, letting her know I'd be coming to Paris.

Christmas was around the corner. Pearl and I had ordered a tree and bought hand-made glass decorations to adorn it with. She had even found a special red silk ribbon for Rex. Everything was on the brink of perfection.

Until now.

I stood on the sidewalk and noticed my hand was trembling. I needed to call Pearl. This news would be the nail in the coffin for me. For us.

I was totally fucked. *Merdre!*

Her cell number was ominously out of order; a voice message saying it was no longer valid. I called her landline in hope.

In dread.

She finally picked up. "Pearl, baby," I said quietly. I could hear the tremors in my voice. "Your cell isn't going through."

"That's because I changed my phone number. It was hacked. By Laura."

"I know."

"What? You *knew* this? Why the hell didn't you warn me?"

"Because I've just found out myself. I'm sorry, I've been a fucking idiot; I can't believe I didn't think of that one, especially in my line of business. I'm so sorry, chérie."

"This is monstrous," she said, her voice cracking. Little did she know the monster had gotten even more out of control.

I swallowed. The lump in my throat barely giving me airspace. "Baby, I've got bad news. I have to go away for a week or so. It's an emergency; I have to see my mother."

"Oh my God, she's not ill, is she?"

"No, nothing like that."

"Are Sophie and Elodie okay?"

"Yes, everyone's fine. Look, I wouldn't be going if it weren't an emergency."

"What, Alexandre? Why aren't you saying what the emergency is?"

"When we're married I'll tell you." As I said those words I realized it came out wrong. Like some sort of moral blackmail. Pearl latched onto that immediately, chewed me out, and then added:

"But what about the holidays?"

"I know, I'm as disappointed as you are."

"Disappointed? That doesn't even begin to describe how I feel, Alexandre. I'm fucking devastated." Pearl rarely swore. "It's our first ever Christmas together."

"I'm in a real bind, baby. A real mess. I need to see my mom.

I don't want to lie to you, chérie, so please don't ask me any more questions."

"You're going to London, aren't you?" Her voice was an ice pick.

"I have no choice."

"We always have a choice, Alexandre. Only abused children or animals, or women who are locked up in a basement some-where, with their passports taken away from them working as slave prostitutes for their sick pimps, or starving people in Africa—they don't have choices, but us? You and I do have choices because we're the lucky ones who live in wealthy western civilizations. We *do* have choices, so don't lay that shit on me."

I listened to Pearl's rant. A knot tightened in my throat. *A choice with a price to pay so high, I'd never forgive myself.* My mind flitted to Pearl being gang raped at college. She didn't have a choice then, although I knew that she was still blaming herself. Those fuckers would get their comeuppance—one of them I'd already tracked down. I thought of Laura again. How she was fucking up everyone's lives. I said in a low voice, "External forces are trying to pull us apart."

"Laura, you mean," Pearl said flatly. Just hearing that woman's name made the apple juice I'd drunk rise in my throat.

"Yes," I admitted, shame caught in my vocal chords.

It was all my fault. That bloody evidence had been sitting happily in a drawer at my mother's in Paris. I brought it to my house in Provence to make sure my stepfather would never find it. To protect my mother. To make her safe. What a fucking joke!

"Laura," Pearl repeated. "You're going to see Laura?"

My internal voice pattered on in my head: *I should have chucked the teeth and hip parts in a river but my mother wanted to keep them as a souvenir to remind her that he was dead. Really dead. My instinct begged me to destroy everything. And I didn't fucking listen.*

"Laura," she said again, annunciating the L.

"Yes," I whispered.

Pearl hung up.

11

I f you asked me to describe Christmas with my mother, or my trip to London to see Laura, or anything about that dark period, I couldn't. It was a gauzy haze of nothingness, like white noise on an old TV screen. I do remember my mantra, *What's yours will come back to you,* and I said this to myself over and over, truly believing it. If Pearl and I were meant to be together, then all this Laura business would somehow sort itself out.

But all that happened was that things got worse.

Laura had stashed the evidence in a safety deposit box at an undisclosed bank. Or so she told me. With a letter saying that if some strange accident befell her, that it would be murder. Names cited. Namely me. She didn't admit to this in so many words, but that was the gist of it. Meanwhile she wanted us to get married.

Or else.

I didn't tell Sophie any of this, and my mother was so distraught that she lay in bed reading romance novels, eating pretzels and drinking white wine, pretending she had the flu, begging me every day by telephone to find a solution.

I called Pearl but of course she never picked up. It seemed she now went about without a cellphone—normal, why would she want Laura tracing her calls? Or me, knowing her every movement? So every now and then, I had a chat on her landline with Daisy or Anthony, who had come to visit her for Christmas. She was fine, they told me, but had no interest of having anything to do with me as long as Laura was in the picture.

I didn't pursue Pearl. How could I until I had a plan up my sleeve? I watched her from afar, though, as she stalked Rex when he went for his walks to Central Park with his 'nanny' Sally. I was stalking her and she was stalking Rex. Ironic. That was what gave me hope. Pearl, Rex and I were a little family unit. We belonged together. I knew that we had a chance when I observed her excitement every time she saw him. I followed her like some sort of detective in a hard-boiled Raymond Chandler novel—keeping my distance, ducking into alleys, lurking behind corners and trees. All I needed was a Fedora hat to complete the look. I had taken to wearing a long, dark, wool, military coat. I wondered what war hero had played his part in it. Did he die on the battlefield or come home triumphant?

I was in my own mini battlefield right now.

An emotional battlefield.

I had become a recluse in my apartment in New York, sporadically going to visit my mother in Paris, or Laura in London, trying to convince her to put an end to her blackmail. She wanted me to father her child. Insane. I was going to give it one more go, I decided. One more go to convince her that her scheme was crazy; that I could never love her child—that the only child I wanted was Pearl's. I had even fantasized about taking Laura heli-skiing, deep sea diving; on some dangerous, life-defying vacation where an accident could happen and nobody could prove a thing. But every time, my mother's face would loom before me, her misting eyes wide, her plea pitiful. She had finally found some peace in her world. I needed to protect her, and the letter Laura spoke of in that safe-deposit box, coupled with the evidence, made the risk too great, although my instinct told me she was bluffing.

The morning was icy and crisp; showing New York City at its most beautiful. Snowflakes drifted through the air as if in slow motion, and an orange glow of sun was casting warm gleams onto the white landscape of Central Park. Dogs were loose, playing and rolling about with each other; their tails up, their owners proud. The dog world going on in the park amused me; the one place where social classes of all ranks could mix happily because they all shared something in common: canines. Park Avenue heiresses and blue collar workers all eyed up their babies, talking of nothing but their dogs' vets visits, eating habits, and quirks. I watched as Pearl and Sally exchanged dialogue and observed Rex, who trotted happily off with Pearl into the depth of the park. I didn't like it the way Pearl was so nonchalant about her own safety. Into the depth of the wood she went, into the Ramble, alone, where some people prowled for anonymous sexual encounters, attracted by the thick cloak of vegetation, serpentine paths, giant boulders and meandering streams.

I followed her, my breath white in the chilled air, my collar up, my boots squeaking on the powdery snow. It made me think of something Pearl said once, and I laughed. "Love is like snow," she told me. "You never know how many inches you're going to get." Inches, in more ways than one, I thought, feeling myself expand inside my jeans the second I set eyes on her. It was insane; just seeing her from afar could get me aroused. And I couldn't deny it now; I was plagued with the idea of never fucking her again. It was driving me to distraction. I couldn't concentrate on work, she was in my dreams, my daydreams—all our lovemaking sessions, both rampant and gentle, were playing and rewinding and playing and rewinding in my sexually deprived, love-obsessed brain. All Laura's talk about my getting her pregnant had done only one thing: make me obsess about getting *Pearl* pregnant. Father her child. The idea of even *touching* Laura was abhorrent to me.

My inner animal was awoken as I watched Pearl now; wearing her little wool hat, her blonde hair peeking out, spread over her shoulders as she held her head up, catching snowflakes on her pink, fresh tongue. I had to kiss her. I wanted her hand to alleviate my aching groin that held so much seed, only for her. Like the park perverts, I stalked her into the wooded area, in hope that she would speak to me—my fantasies had me fucking her against a tree. My cock flexed again, imaging how sweet that would be—I could feel that rod of mine pining for attention, eager to fulfill its biological role.

I was the prowler and Pearl my prey.

"Pearl!" I shouted after her. She carried on walking. Rex was darting in and out of scrubby groves, chasing squirrels. "Pearl, stop!" I hurried up to her and closed my hand around her coated elbow. I pulled her towards me and wrapped my arms around her. I rested my head against hers and breathed into her mouth, my breath hot, my desire scorching. She pulled her face away from mine and shot me a disdainful look.

"Why are you following me like this? What do you want?" Her eyes were darts.

She knew what I wanted, and she wanted it too, although her head was telling her to disbelieve her heart. I needed *all* of her, every single inch of her: her mind, her body, her sweet, kind soul. I pulled her into me again and could hear a growl rumble from within myself. I wished I had more self-control. I pressed myself up against her, holding her hips into my hard groin with one hand and her shoulder with the other. I began to kiss her all over her face, the melting snowflakes soft on my lips, the smell of her skin like honey as I inhaled her scent. I maneuvered her so she was up against a tree, my tongue parting her mouth as I probed my own inside, flickering it, letting it tangle with hers. She moaned and I imagined her wet pussy pulsating with yearning for me. Another wave of desire surged through me, coupled with visions of fatherhood, and I groaned into her lips.

"Leave me alone, you bastard," she breathed into my mouth as she whimpered through the kiss. "Oh, God, Alexandre, why can't you leave me alone?"

"I need you, baby," I whispered, rubbing my groin against her. All she had to do to make me come was brush her hand against my crotch—I was that horny, but she didn't. I took off my glove on my right hand and slipped my palm through her coat, around the flesh on her waist, forcing it down her belly and down into her panties. I slid my finger along her slit and felt the oozing wet warmth—but only for a second before she pushed my hand away with a thud. I slipped it behind, onto her ass and up to the small of her back. I wanted to feel those little dimples there, but she slammed her butt back against the tree, trapping my hand.

"Fuck you, Alexandre Chevalier, who do you think you *are* molesting me like this?"

"You're mine," I growled, clawing the ass that belonged to me. "I have to have you, I can't stand this anymore. You and I belong together, Pearl. Every waking moment, every sleeping second, I'm thinking about you, baby, dreaming about you. I'm so crazy and obsessed with you, it hurts."

"You just want to fuck me and go back to Laura, that skinny 'asparagus stick', as Sophie so brilliantly described her. Keep away from me, Alexandre—stop torturing me with your games!"

But her protestation was fruitless as her frail arms tried to beat on my heaving chest. I kissed her nose, her eyes, her chin, her hair, then back to her full, soft lips. I murmured into her mouth, "I love you Pearl, I love you more than you can possibly know; my life is an empty shell without you. It means nothing without you by my side."

"You want to have your cake and eat it too," she objected into my kiss.

"You're—" I trailed my tongue along her lips— "the only cake I want, I swear. The sweetest cake there is." It was true— she smelled delicious; her skin more fragrant than ever; not perfume but her own Pearlish scent that was indescribable. It sent shivers of lust and love right down my spine, pounding into my dick—all a mélange of beautiful, confusing chaos of love.

The drama carried on, the banter about Laura as I tried to protest my innocence in vain. I told Pearl that Laura had something I needed, which only blew her fire to flare up into a full-on bonfire—I could not slake her fury. There was a new, defiant look in her eye as if she were protecting something more than just her pride. I wasn't going to get my way, although I was trying damn hard.

"You and Laura deserve each other," Pearl hissed, her breath a mist that caught my tongue mid-sentence.

"Pearl, please, we—"

"You two," a voice from behind me yelled. "No sex in public, it's a felony." It was a police officer, strolling toward us, half amused, half serious. I stepped back; Pearl ducked from under me, slipping from my grip. She ran off, trammeling fresh snow, Rex racing after her, his deep paw prints testament of his adoration for her.

Even Rex was against me or he would have stayed loyal by my side. I felt wrath swell in my heart—the kind I experienced in the Foreign Legion, because I felt a sense of hopelessness; that the world was outside of my control. Destiny taking its own pigheaded course. I needed to expel the pent-up energy spiraling though my veins. I needed sex to calm me. That obviously wasn't going to happen.

So I needed to fight.

That rapist fuck had had it coming to him for nearly twenty years.

Payback time.

12

The muscle memory was about to kick in again. In a trance, I drove to Mystic where one of the guys who'd raped Pearl lived on weekends. His house, where he was cozily ensconced with his wife and kids, was pretty plush. I'd had him tracked down; and found out everything I needed to know. Revenge was bubbling, like Laura's cauldron, in my hot veins. It was my way of showing Pearl how much I loved her, although I wasn't going to reveal my violent side to her. No, this 'escapade' would be my secret.

I followed him to his drinking hole by the waterfront and took him by surprise. It felt good to scare the living shit out of him, even though I did it with a fake gun; one of those cigarette lighters. He had raped my girl, albeit eighteen years ago. He had defiled her with his stinking dick. I hated mankind. Man, not kind. Man—so often a fucking piece of shit. Pearl and Natalie were right to expose all those fucks in their documentaries—

merciless nothings who were ruining women's lives in such a cavalier way. I felt so proud of Pearl. She had that all-consuming sense of justice. She was a fighter. A warrior. She wanted to right the world. This was my chance to help her.

Few people have guts to do what she did for a living. Everyone is so busy trying to seek approval, be popular, be 'liked' on Facebook or HookedUp. Pearl didn't care about being liked. She cared about integrity. She was on a mission to defend others through her job as documentary producer, but somehow, she hadn't believed that she, herself, needed shielding. This was my way of protecting her, albeit too late. I enjoyed laying a few punches into this overweight, ex-football-playing cocksucker, swinging my leg hard into his chest—letting him know that he had fucked (literally) with the wrong person.

He'd fucked my girl. In the nastiest, most despicable way. Which meant he'd also fucked me.

Revenge is a dish best served cold. And this revenge had been on ice for eighteen years.

I remember two distinct things about that night in Mystic: the cold. And the man's expression on his milky white face when I told him he'd have to part with two month's salary—a hundred grand to be wired to a charity I'd set up in Pearl's name. In 'Jane Doe's' name. With a ten percent discount if he revealed all his rapist buddies' names—each and every one who participated in the gang rape that fateful night. Of all the punches and kicks, the financial punch was the most painful to this pathetic man; hit 'em where it hurts most—in the wallet.

It gave me momentary satisfaction.

But it reminded me of Pearl's vulnerability. She needed to be protected. She needed me by her side, whether she knew it or not.

I couldn't stand to be without her a second more. Despite my promises to my mother, I'd have to tell Pearl the truth because I was dying inside.

I left Mystic and drove back to New York, singing along with the car radio to the Kinks, *You Really Got Me*. I had to make Pearl mine, whatever it took. *You got me so I can't sleep at night…*so true.

Sleep…it was hitting me now. I pulled the car over. I felt spent and needed five minutes shut-eye before I continued driving—I didn't want to have an accident through tiredness. The image of Pearl had me needing to jack off—to expel the heat I felt inside after the fight. I had blood on my knuckles, a bruised lip; the idea of her kissing it better made my cock swell with longing. I came fast and hard, her tits and ass on rewind and play, rewind and play, as I raced myself to an intense orgasm. Better this way—I needed to see her and didn't want to behave like a feral animal, the way I had in Central Park. Now I was less frenetic. I closed my eyes, calmer now, reclined the leather seat, and drifted off into a brief but heavy catnap.

"Don't fucking move." One hand is clamped on my neck. His breathing is heaving fast and furious, his nails like bear's claws digging into me. His other hand is pulling down my pajama bottoms. Am I dreaming? I open my eyes wide and try to roll forward but he's got me in a tight grip. I jab my elbow backwards and it whacks into his shoulder but I can't escape. Maman is in the hospital for the night. Because of him. Yesterday, I attacked him, trying to protect her, and he left the apartment, saying he wouldn't ever return, muttering under his whiskey breath as Maman lay in a pool of blood

on the kitchen floor. I dialed the fire brigade because the ambulance is always too slow.

I didn't hear him come in tonight. I didn't bolt the door from inside, in case Sophie came home late. Stupid me. I'm all alone. He's naked. He smells of sweat and whiskey.

"I said don't fucking move or it'll hurt." I hear him grab his bottle and slug down the booze. I take the moment to slither out from his grip but it makes him roar. "Why can't you just let me love you, goddamn it? You're my son; I love you."

I hop to my bedroom door—my pajamas are around my ankles so I can't move fast—I can't open the door in time. He chases me, tackling me like a rugby player. We both fall with a thud to the ground.

"Papa, please, you're drunk. Let me go!" I crawl up on my knees. I'm panting hard but he pushes me down on the floor again. My teeth smash against my lips. I'm bleeding. "Please, Papa," I beg, my face crushed on the black and white tiled linoleum. I thrash like a snake but he holds me down. My pajamas are still caught around my ankles like a net. He's sticking it in and it hurts. I scream out in pain and manage to get to my knees so it slips out.

"Stop jiggling about, Alexandre Dubois—stop disobeying your father!"

I roll on my side. I'm on my back now. I take his arm, bring my mouth up to his shoulder and bite into it with all the power I have.

"Ah! You fuck!" he cries out in a blood-curdling yell. He gets up and staggers towards his whiskey bottle, grabs it and races at me, swinging it wildly. My hand is on the doorknob and I turn it. The door is ajar; it's open. I stick my barefoot in the gap but I'm too late. He smashes the bottle against the door. I shove my head through—whiskey spills all over my back. I feel a thump on my bottom and see blood pooling on the floor. My bottom is stinging as the whiskey trickles between my crack. It's my blood I see. He

jams the broken bottle inside me, twisting it like a corkscrew and I'm screaming in pain now. Shards of glass, whiskey, blood—my blood—all over the floor. I hear a noise. I look up and see Sophie rushing towards me. She's clutching a kitchen knife—

I sat bolt upright with a jerk. Jesus! I was lying on something sticking right into my butt. My wallet. I let out the breath that I had been holding in without realizing. That memory hadn't been around for a while. Why now? I thought of the guy's blood tonight in Mystic, pooling around his ears after I struck him with my ruthless kick. I remembered my own blood, the glass, the metallic taste in my mouth, my chipped tooth, my father with the knife stuck in his groin, and how Sophie and I ran and ran and never returned.

Maman had a choice and she chose *him*. After everything, she betrayed us. I sat there now in the rental car, my head slumped on the steering wheel and choked back the lump in my throat. *I will not be broken. I will not be broken.* Finally, I had my chance at happiness with Pearl but I was jeopardizing it all for a woman who had not protected me, who had not put me before her own desires. I couldn't shoulder her weight any longer. I needed to be honest with Pearl. Or I would lose her. I *had* lost her. But maybe, just maybe, I could win her back. If.

If I told her the whole story.

She needed to know who and what my mother really was.

I slipped into Pearl's rental apartment—I still hadn't handed over my set of keys. Daisy and Amy and Pearl would probably, I deduced, be asleep by now, and I didn't want to wake anyone. But Pearl was wide-awake, a tub of ice cream in one hand and one of Amy's toy cowboy pistols in the other. I fell in love with her all over again. It was proof that we had to be together; that we were soul mates. Both wielding toy guns in the same night?

It was a *fait accompli*.

She was standing there in her pajama bottoms, her tits voluptuous, her nipples erect in her little tank. But sex was no longer on my mind. I was too broken up that night.

"Why are you doing this Alexandre? Why are you here? Back to torture me?"

"Love the toy gun," I said with a faint smile. "You and I have more in common than you think, baby." But it wasn't funny anymore. I crumpled to the ground, my resilience in fragments, my barriers gone. A tear plopped onto the floor, landing on the slush of snow pooled next to my big black boots. "I can't stand this anymore, Pearl. I really can't." I looked up at her like a puppy waiting for a clue from his mistress. I had no answers. I needed help.

This was the moment in time when everything froze like a snowflake floating in midair; unique and perfect. I gave in to Pearl. Completely. I threw myself into the arms of Fate. If God gave a fuck, he'd sort this Laura shit out for us, but nothing was now going to stand in the way of the goddamn truth, my mother included.

I took Pearl home, just as she was, in her pajamas. We didn't make love but we did make promises. I told her everything— each tiny, gruesome detail, leaving nothing unsaid. She embraced my truth, swore she'd stand by my side, no matter what. We were a team, she said, and nothing could break that.

Recounting how my mom murdered my father in the bathtub, by throwing a live electric heater into the water, somehow alleviated me of the black weight I had been heaving over my shoulder for so many years. Just saying the words made me a free man.

I kissed Pearl's knuckles on her ringed hand and said—the diamond glittering in my eyes as I spoke—"Pearl, I know you and I know myself. If we don't spend the rest of our days together we won't be truly happy. We'll go around half dead. Without you, my flame is snuffed out. Without you, I am only half a man. Without you, my life will be running on empty." Maybe I sounded like a cliché—an actor speaking his lines—but it was unrehearsed and how I truly felt.

I came clean with Pearl that night. I revealed all to her. My past. My mother. The lot. And then Pearl told me *her* big secret. The best damn secret known to man.

She was pregnant with my child.

13

I won't go into detail about all the trials and tribulations that Pearl and I endured over the next month or so because of Laura. Suffice it to say that there was enough madness and intrigue to make a long movie (that would have seemed too far-fetched for most intelligent beings) *and* a TV spin-off of several seasons, to boot. Laura had us running around in circles, doing cartwheels, backward walkovers, and nosedives, suffering several near coronaries and many sleepless nights. But the difference now, was that Pearl and I weathered the storm *together.* And knowing that she was pregnant made our family unit stronger, all the more invincible. A tiny voice inside my head assured me that we would pull thorough.

We had to.

We had a thousand nutty plans to out-fox Laura. Her latest scheme was to use me as a sperm donor for her brainchild baby-to-be, generously letting Pearl 'keep' me for herself, Laura having finally given up on actually marrying me. It was bordering on laughable her plan was so outlandish.

Our last 'encounter' was at Laura's house in Chelsea. She was threatening my mother again and I found myself on a plane to London to put an end to her blackmail, once and for all. However, in an unexpected twist, Fate and Irony got their first.

Laura had an accident—another fall, this time tumbling downstairs in her own house, her head cracking open, and her heart—which had erroneously believed it loved me—finally stopped beating.

Her husband James (emerging like a dormouse from a long winter) had been in rehab for several months—all this I found out during the bizarre scene that followed.

Pearl had been imagining all that time that Laura had topped him off. James was one of those high-class heroin addicts (able to afford the best) and had spent time at The Priory—a sort of British Betty Ford equivalent—to kick his habit. Although, I didn't find all this out until we were both embedded in a drama that made us both look like murderers.

James and I found ourselves in an almost comical situation— murder suspects as we were—as we both observed Laura lying, dead as a smashed mosquito, at the bottom of the staircase in their London house. We arrived at the scene of the 'crime' simultaneously.

She had a serene smile on her lipsticked lips as if the accident really had taken her unawares. I still remember the color red, vivid and dramatic—the pool of blood, the crimson of her silky negligee, her shiny, vermillion-painted lips. Both James and I looked guilty as dogs who had raided the trash—I had just come in through the back, via the garage door (with my own set of keys), and James suddenly emerged from the front door. Which one of us was a victim of circumstance, and which one a murderer? We fixed our gaze, first on Laura, and then one another.

"She must have careened down the stairs like a sled," I said to James as we continued to size each other up. We then looked back down at Laura's corpse, each silently accusing the other. "Her feet must have slipped forward, and her body slanting backwards, bashing her head on the bottom step." *Jesus, it sounds as if I know too much.*

James cast his glance at one dainty-heeled slipper on Laura's left foot and then looked about to find its pair. It was lying a few feet away. He bent down and touched her pale cheek and I thought, "Fuck it's *him*; *he* did it." Laura looked all tarted-up; make-up, a sexy, skimpy little outfit—for my benefit? James obviously thought so, and by the look on his face he suspected his wife and I were having an affair. *He killed her out of jealousy and rage*, I thought.

I locked my eyes with his.

"You fucking cunt," James shrieked at me. "You sneaky fucking bastard." He laid his palm across his wife's breast to double-check if she was as dead as she looked. "You bloody well killed my wife!"

"James, no! What are you saying? That's *crazy*. I just *got* here, at the same time you were coming through the front door. I swear. This is just as much a surprise for me as it is for you."

James looked up at me with his odd, angular face, a sneer etched on his thin lips. He raked his bony hand through his blond hair and said in his British, upper-class voice:

"What I don't understand, is why. *Why,* Alexandre? Did you try to kill her last time, too? When she had that supposed 'accident' and she ended up in a bloody wheelchair? I mean, it's obvious she fell down the stairs. One push, that's all it must have taken. You fucking bastard!" Spittle sprayed as he spoke.

I knew he wasn't the type to lay a punch. English aristocratic men are usually pretty cowardly (too polite for their own good), but I flinched all the same, and wiped his spray of angry spittle from my face. My stomach churned with sick dread as I thought of my father's teeth and hip bits—evidence in that safety deposit box. Laura dead was all I fucking needed.

I shouted out, "Okay, James…this is just great. You accusing me of murder? How about I accuse *you?* Where the fuck have you been for the last couple of months? Eh? Suddenly appearing like this. Perhaps you *knew* that I was coming over. Laura knew. I called her. Maybe it was really bloody convenient for you to bump her off and then blame me."

"I'm going to call the police," James spluttered, his eyes wet with emotion. Real emotion? Fake?

The word 'police' sent a hammer to my heart. I thought of the evidence. Laura's note stowed with her lawyer revealing everything if she ever had an accident. My mother rotting in a jail somewhere. And I'd be accused of her murder, on top of it all. Fuck!

James traced his finger along Laura's once-determined jaw. "Laura wouldn't just fall down her own stairs in her own house now, would she?"

"It is possible, she had those heeled slippers on," I answered.

"How the fuck did you get in, anyway?"

111

"Through the back, from the garden," I said. "I still have your garage keys."

James nodded. "That's right—your Aston Martin. I'd forgotten about that."

Now I looked even guiltier. My Aston Martin excuse wouldn't wash because it wasn't fucking there anymore! Suresh, my driver, had moved it to France. I had no reason, *whatsoever*, for coming through the back door. I quickly added, "Actually, I moved my car a while ago. I knocked on the front door but there was no answer, and Laura didn't pick up the phone. She was expecting me. So I came through the back."

"Nice excuse, Alex. Tell that to Scotland bloody Yard."

That particular TV episode was a long and complicated one— the finale to an outrageously elaborate plot, peppered with an element of black humor. I must have had 'killer' written all over my face, because I could not deny the onslaught of fatalistic fantasies I'd had in the run-up to Laura's death. I do think I willed it to happen. I really do. The power of imagination is awesome. And when I say 'awesome' I mean it in the true sense of the word.

In my mind I had killed Laura. Perhaps James had too; who knew the anger that had been building inside him. Here we were, staring at each other open-mouthed, dumbstruck that she really was gone for good—each accusing the other of murder. It was as if the screenwriters in our TV serial spin-off had Agatha Christie in mind, because what ensued, after we had both been arrested on suspicion of murder, was that Laura and James's housekeeper, Mrs. Blake, came forward.

As I sat at the local police station, wondering how I would

burrow my way out of my Alice-In-Wonderland rabbit hole, Mrs. Blake—my fairy godmother—waved her magic wand: waxy polish on the stairs, coupled with Laura's kitten-heeled slippers, were both the murder weapons and the murderers rolled into one. It was confirmed by forensics that there was polish all over the soles of Laura's shoes.

Finally, Pearl and I were free.

Or so I thought.

Because Laura—even from her *chaise longue* in Hell (she was probably having cocktails and flirting with the Devil himself)—had other plans for our future.

14

Our long-awaited wedding was a fairytale. It took place in Lapland—yes, Lapland really does exist—on St. Valentine's Day itself.

Pearl had done everything to make it extraordinary, including reindeer with white velvet ribbons tied around their antlers, to pull us with sleds. She had told little Amy that they were on loan from Santa Claus and even I believed her. It really was a dream winter wedding. Pearl was the Ice Queen and I her King. She looked resplendent in a floor-length, ivory-colored gown. It was silk velvet, and caught the light as she glided through the wedding ceremony, the long train trailing behind her. Beads of 'ice crystal' blossoms cascaded off one shoulder. Elodie and Amy were her bridesmaids, both dressed in pink. Elodie looked like a movie star, the derriere of her gown low and scooped, caught at the back with pink silk roses, and Amy, taking her role very seriously, was dressed in a pink, baby-doll, organza number with a wreath in her hair.

The chapel was made of real ice, sculpted from the frozen land. Dozens of artists had arrived from across the globe to carve the ice interiors. Each year, they told us, the designs were completely different and would melt in springtime. Nothing but our memories and photographs would be testament to our magical day.

I stood there in my tails, nervously waiting for Pearl as she walked quietly down the aisle. Everybody was entranced. Sophie was misty-eyed; both her husband and Alessandra by her side— he still had no idea, and thought Alessandra was just an old friend from Sophie's 'acting' days. My mother stood tall and proud, my stepfather holding her hand. Anthony and Daisy were blatantly blubbing into handkerchiefs. And Pearl's father winked at me as if to say, *She's yours now, don't fuck up the way I did.*

No, I wasn't going to fuck-up. I had fought hard for this prize.

I locked my eyes with Pearl's and let out a sigh of relief. She was about to be mine. All mine. I thought back to how she bolted from me at Van Nuys Airport and wondered, just for a split second, if she would run from me now. But her gaze remained steadily on my face, a faint smile on her lips. Concentrated. Determined. She wanted me. All of me. The bad me, the okay me, the me that knew that we would be together as long as we both lived.

A dysfunctional match made in Heaven.

No, she wasn't any more perfect than I was—in fact, she really was a pretty wayward character, but she was perfect for *me*. She broke out in a huge smile and I beamed at her in return. We giggled nervously like schoolchildren at the excitement of it all. Then I mouthed silently, "Pearl Chevalier," as she walked slowly towards me, her eyes glistening, twinkling with emotion.

And then she was by my side as we did our wedding vows. At the end, after we'd exchanged rings, the pastor asked everyone to affirm our matrimony.

"If you believe that Pearl and Alexandre are made for one another, say yes!" he cried out, and everyone shouted back in unison, "Yes!"

"Say it louder!" he demanded, and they did. It was an unorthodox touch on his part, no doubt planned ahead, but it took us both by surprise, and something about that big 'Yes' made us snap out of the surreal dream of our fairytale wedding, and into a shocking moment. Shocking because this was it. Forever—the Yes giving us strength for our future. They all believed in us, just as much as *we* believed in us. Words are powerful when spoken by many at one time. Especially with conviction.

It was comforting to know that our twins were also part of the ceremony, even if only in Pearl's stomach. The family I had always dreamed of was almost complete.

Our wedding bands were made of 22 carat gold and each had the other's name inscribed inside. So not only was *PEARL* engraved on my heart, but on my finger, too.

The celebration continued all night, everybody doing their own thing—sled rides, vodka drinking, feasting, and general jovialities all round. I just wanted to be alone with Pearl.

I helped her down from the sled onto the powdery, glittery snow, as snowflakes fluttered onto our faces. Reindeer and sled dropped us off at our remote log cabin where a glowing fire awaited us inside. I glanced skyward, soaking up the spectacle. The Aurora Borealis—the Northern Lights—swooped above us. Five fingers of sweeping green light, like a giant's hand, raised itself towards the Heavens. God's hand? Pearl thought so. If ever there was a moment when I felt that there was a Higher Power, this was it. I had it all. The woman I loved by my side, pregnant with twins, and a sense of freedom and relief as I had never known before in my life. The old world was behind me and I was starting afresh. We were a mountain together, Pearl and I.

That night, we fucked for the first time in months, so it really did feel to me as if it was new to us. Okay, we'd had delicious sex in many other ways, but no penetration—doctor's orders in case Pearl suffered a miscarriage. It had happened to her twice before during her marriage to Saul and we didn't want to take any risks. So this night really was our wedding night in every sense. She was my virgin bride. I felt reverent towards my new wife, but I also couldn't wait to enter her. Deep. Profound. I needed that union. It had been far too long. As beautiful as her wedding gown was, I had visions of what lay beneath—and I couldn't wait.

I observed Pearl quietly as she lay on the bed before me. Horny as I was, I didn't want to rush a thing. This was a moment to be savored for the rest of our lives. I could hardly breathe I had so much love overflowing from within me; a pumping surge which took my body by surprise. I could now know *for sure* that she belonged to me. No more ifs or buts. No more cat and mouse.

"Pearl Chevalier," I said, rolling those sweet words on my tongue. "Madame Pearl Chevalier, tu es magnifique." The golden light of the fire highlighted the curves of her nude body and glowed on her beautiful face. "Je t'aime," I added with pride. I could feel myself get hard. "Do you realize how I've been longing for this moment? Counting down the days, the hours?"

"Well, that's how they had to do it in the olden days. The groom had to *wait* for his wedding night," she said.

I remained stationary, drinking in the incomparable image. The image that I wanted imprinted on my brain until the end of my days, so when I was old, gray and doddery I could remember this moment.

"Do you know what I'm going to do to you?" I murmured. She bit her lip and spread her legs a touch. My cock flexed again. I slowly sauntered towards her, my eyes locked with hers. Her blonde hair had grown in the last few months and was spread like silky bands across her shoulders.

I bent down and kissed her. I inhaled in her sweet scent, and a feral moan rumbled from my throat. She opened her lips and her pink tongue, fresh and eager, darted out to meet mine. She whimpered and I knew how wet she'd be, even though I hadn't even touched that part of her yet. "Pearl Chevalier," I said again, and winked at her. "Mrs. Pearl Chevalier. Madame Pearl Chevalier."

"Oh don't be so sure, I might decide to be Mzzzz," she teased, "or mademoiselle. I might keep my maiden name."

"No more games, Pearl," I said, nipping her pussycat lip, "you're mine now."

"Prove it," she moaned into my mouth.

"Oh, I will."

Her nipples were tweaked with desire and her tits full and round from the pregnancy. I trailed my tongue over her lips, and my fingers grazed across her taut breasts and I pinched and rolled one nipple lightly. "Oh God," she groaned, her eyes fluttering.

I pinned her beneath me, my knees either side of her hips, my cock rock-hard against her curved belly where Louis and Madeleine—we had just come up with the names a couple of hours earlier—were growing stronger day by day. I almost felt wicked, knowing I was about to defile their pure mother. But it also made me all the more ravenous for Pearl, knowing that the seed inside her was growing into two special little beings, who would talk and walk and have their own opinions about life. *We* had created them together. Through love. And lust.

She traced her fingers over my pecs and ran them slowly down to my abdomen, letting her fingers dip into the ridges, scanning my torso with her guileless, approving eyes. "You're beautiful, Alexandre," she told me.

I leaned down to kiss her again, letting our lips rest quietly together. We were united and about to be joined even closer. I needed that proximity. I needed to be deep inside her. I edged further down until my cock rested on her slick wetness. Desire pooled low in my gut and blood pumped hard and fast into my groin. I was huge and worried that I might hurt her, yet the need to fuck her was stronger than ever. I could feel every nuance of her soft, liquid heat and I slid in just a millimeter. *Fuck!* It felt out of this world. "Is that okay, baby? I don't want to damage you."

"Help me," she whimpered.

"Am I hurting you?"

"Please fuck me, Alexandre. *Please.*" I pushed in another inch, using my arms to control my weight on her. Her eyes flicked to my biceps and she bit her lip. She bucked her hips up at me to get closer but I carried on controlling myself. "Your muscles are so defined," she whispered. "You're so incredible—every part of you."

I made small circular movements so she could adjust to my size. I could feel myself throbbing, and the sensation of her tight pussy, like a warm glove, had my sensitive cock ready to plunge into her. Fuck her hard. But I counted to ten and remained steadily, gently thrusting, only a couple of inches in. I had to control myself.

"So. Juicy. So. Fucking. Beautiful." My dick punctuated each word.

She clawed my ass with her nails and drew me in closer but I wouldn't give in, in case I hurt her. Her ankles clamped my calves and she pumped herself in rhythm with me. "Oh my God, this is incredible," she moaned. "I'm going to come soon."

Our foreheads were locked together and our breaths in unison as if we were one being. I pulled out and let my cock slide up and down her clit—she was on the edge—so this was a way to both bring her back down and also to drive her wild. I wanted this to last longer because I was in a sort of spiritual, lovemaking bliss. She was too. Long gone were the days when I had to work hard to make Pearl come—that challenge was over. I slipped back inside her and resumed the mini thrusts, just my crown teasing her mercilessly as she arched her back, groaning for more of my thick, solid cock.

"Remember to...Love. Honor. And, Obey. Your. Husband," I growled, half jesting. I could feel her contractions gripping me, sucking me in—she was coming hard. I couldn't hold it any longer. I pushed myself in a little more and exploded, my seed probably joining the twins.

Pearl's tongue was all over mine as she murmured almost incoherently, "I'll obey you, Alexandre. I'll do anything for you. Anything—every inch of me belongs to you."

We were climaxing together in an emotional rush of trust, lust and love.

"Anything?"

"Oh God I'm still coming….anything, baby," she moaned, her fingers were gripping my ass.

"Stay with me forever, my belle Pearl."

"I swear," she said, kissing me again.

15

Pearl and I settled beautifully into married life. After the twins were born, she became more of a woman and less of a girl; so much so that I would goad her sometimes to be more frivolous and less responsible. Perhaps I missed that foolish character that jumped out of the ladies' room window and got me running round in circles—a little bit anyway. I understood that our wayward paths had been the right ones, and nothing we had ever done in our lives could—or should—have been different, including the 'fuck-ups.' If they had been, we wouldn't have felt so lucky to be together.

Pearl became quite a mover and shaker with HookedUp Enterprises and began to spread her wings. I was so proud. Those wings which had been damaged when I first knew her, were now helping her soar to great heights. She had so much more confidence being married and a mother.

One evening, as we sat by a roaring fire in our apartment, I came clean about the Bloody Mary incident—it had been eating at me. I didn't want to hide anything. I went into detail about how I was trussed up like a Christmas turkey, hands bound with electric cable, 'marinated' by the drug-spiked Bloody Mary, with Laura poised on top of me, my dick ready for lift-off. Pearl thought it hilarious—in retrospect—but admitted that I'd done the right thing not to tell her at the time. We had no secrets from each other now. I reveled in my newfound freedom of not carrying weights upon my shoulders; secrets so heavy that they made you stumble through life—what a relief. Both Pearl and I were free and it felt fucking great.

I had become a sort of househusband, being able to work from home, with the twins on my lap, or crawling about the floor while I 'tested' the video games in my new company, or made calls—I'd also bought up a chain of boutique hotels to add to my portfolio, which I needed to manage. Sally had become nanny to the children as well as to Rex, so we were a busy, bustling household. We were making ridiculous money with our video games, my new partner and I, and it was more creative than HookedUp, which Sophie was now handling pretty much solo. I still owned shares but was out of the day-to-day grind of it. Sebastian's and my new video game was a work of art, with high concept character building and role-play. Meanwhile, Pearl and Natalie went from strength to force with HookedUp Enterprises and had branched out into magazines as well.

The evening of the New York premiere of *Stone Trooper* had

finally arrived. Originally, Pearl had said that I needn't bother accompanying her, but then she changed her mind. She had assumed I agreed but I was getting so into the househusband thing, I had other ideas. I lay on the sofa with my toddlers crawling all over me, their sticky fingers in my eyes and hair.

"Alexandre, you *have* to come," Pearl pleaded, standing at the doorway. Her blonde hair was swept up in an elegant chignon—the hairdresser had been in our apartment all day. Her make-up was sultry and darkly seductive. She looked stunning.

"Sorry, babe, I really don't like doing red carpet—you know that," I mumbled, a set of baby fingers in my mouth.

"But this is different."

"Still red carpet. I like to keep my anonymity. I already did the first premiere in LA. One's enough. Sophie will be with you. Natalie, Alessandra, Elodie. You really don't need me as well. Besides, someone has to stay home with Louis and Madeleine, and Sally's busy tonight."

"You told me Sally would be here," Pearl grumbled. "You're so stubborn, you know that? So *tetu*, it's unbelievable!"

"I'll stay home, order Chinese, and hang out with the twins."

She walked towards me slowly, letting her ivory silk robe fall open. My eyes grew greedy observing her beautiful nude body—freshly moisturized—she smelled of peaches or something sweet and edible. Her tits were still big from breastfeeding. I felt myself go instantly hard. I'd fuck those tits later. Maybe now even, while she was all perfect—I'd ravage her—*women hate it when you mess with their hair and make-up*. I winked at her.

She raised her brow. "Alright, fine, don't come. Don't blame me if guys come on to me tonight. Don't blame me if Mikhail what's-his-face eyes me up and flirts his ass off."

She had my attention. "That Russian arms dealer fuck? What's he doing coming to our premiere?"

"Oh, it's suddenly *our* premiere, is it? A moment ago I was on my own."

"Seriously, who invited him?"

She exited the room with a *Wouldn't-you-like-to-know* look on her face.

I got up from the sofa, Louis in one arm, Madeleine in the other. Their eyes followed Pearl too, and Louis gurgled, with a grin on his face as if he found the whole scenario hilarious. I called after her, "Who invited him?"

I took out my cell and arranged a babysitter, there and then. Jeanine, in fact, who worked at HookedUp Enterprises with Pearl. She was a big fan of Louis and Madeleine. She said 'yes' immediately. I called Sally for backup and when she said no, I made her an offer she couldn't refuse.

The *Stone Trooper* premiere was less of a flashy affair than LA, but still, everyone seemed to want to be there to be seen, rather than to see.

Not Pearl, though. She was in professional mode, politely chatting to everyone who was congratulating her as we made our torturously slow way up the red carpet, toward the open doors of the movie theatre. She had on a floor-length silk chiffon gown that trailed and shimmied behind her—a sort of pale gold that made her angelic, although she was unaware of how dazzling she looked. It was amazing how fast she'd lost the post-pregnancy weight. Swimming, I guessed. Except for her breasts—no weight lost there. It unnerved me to know that others might see that too. As we ambled on through to the screening—she glided, I ambled—Elodie came up behind me, her eyes flashing with anger.

She clutched my elbow. "What the fuck?" she seethed in a hoarse whisper.

I had the twins on my mind and was on autopilot, nodding politely at people but not paying attention to what anyone said. "What? Did someone tread on your gown?" I asked absentmindedly. But Elodie wasn't wearing a gown. She was back to Goth mode. She wore spiked black heels that could poke out an eye, and skin-tight leggings with a see-through top. Luckily, she had on some sort of bra underneath.

"She's gay, isn't she? She's fucking well gay!" She shot a look at her mother, who was walking by Alessandra's side, her hips pressed close to her girlfriend. As was often the case, Elodie's father was absent. Maybe he was having an affair too. He was rarely around for events, or if he was, he had an air of invisibility.

"Your mother?" I said. There was no point pretending otherwise. I was amazed it had taken Elodie so long to work it out.

She pinched my arm. "Thanks for warning me. Thanks for hiding it from me for all this time."

"Elodie, this isn't the moment. Come over tomorrow and we'll talk about it."

"Oh crap, that's all I fucking need," she sneered. I looked over to her line of vision and saw the Russian. He was making a beeline for us.

I turned to her. "You know him, Elodie?"

"You could say that."

For a second, the man looked as if he were about to slit my throat in front of the whole crowd, but then he suddenly smiled as if he recognized me.

"Alexandre Chevalier," he said, his accent very pronounced. "What a pleasure." He held out his right hand. I felt some cameras flash.

I didn't reciprocate. I replied coldly, "I'm sorry but we don't know each other."

Elodie rolled her eyes. "Uncle Alexandre, this is Mikhail Prokovich, Mikhail, my uncle, Alexandre," she said in a bored drawl.

His eyes were menacing as he raked his gaze over her. He said in French, "You can do better than that, Elodie, my darling. Especially considering I'm your date."

"*Va te faire foutre*," she retorted, storming off towards the doors to go inside.

That's right, va te faire foutre—fuck you, asshole! My heart sank into my stomach. My *darling?* Her *date? What the hell?* My eyes locked with his. "You *know* my niece?"

He smirked at me and answered cockily, again in French, "I more than know her. I'm *fucking* her."

Before my brain was even aware of what I was doing, my fist—as if it had a will of its own—punched the man's face. He tumbled backwards. My leg swung in a high arch, landing on the side of his chest in a hard thud. But he didn't fall. I could hear gasps and women squealing with fright. The fuck shook himself off like a Spanish bull and came toward me, hurling his full weight at me. He was as tall as I was and strongly built, his chest wide, his arms thick—even though he was wearing a suit, I could tell he worked out.

Pearl screamed, "Alexandre, stop! What are you doing?" *Good point*, I thought. *What am I doing?* My limbs seemed to have their own agenda.

"I told you I don't do red carpet well," I said—a James Bond quip if ever there was one—as I dodged to the side, managing to avoid Mikhail Prokovich's heaving torso lunge right at me. "Step back, Pearl," I urged her, realizing this was so not the time, nor the place, for this fiasco—that I should have kept my cool.

But it was too late. The guy twisted his body at the last minute and caught me in a vice, his arm clamped about my middle. He was a tough fucker, seemed to have been trained in some sort of martial art like I was, because he had some sneaky moves—I'd met my match.

"She's only nineteen, you fuck!" I hissed at him as we wrestled, both trying to overpower the other, without making too much of a scene. But we *were* making a scene. And how. The next thing I knew, Pearl was beating him on the head with her purse. I pleaded, "Pearl, you must step *back*, chérie, you'll get hurt," although my love for her at that moment swelled, not only at her bravery, but because of her loyalty.

A bright flash blinded me for a second. The paparazzi were at it in full swing now—snapping away at the spectacle: two grown men fighting in public. And then the Russian's large knee jerked up and smashed me in the balls. I winced in pain, doubling forward. Prokovich jabbed me in the back with his sharp elbow. I used my crouched position to my advantage and, bending down even further, I hooked my fingers about his ankle. My opponent lost his balance and fell backwards to the floor, landing unceremoniously on his shoulder.

"You fuck!" he yelled up at me. I wiped my forehead—fighting in a suit was not the most comfortable option, and perspiration was gathering on my brow.

I leered down at him as he was getting up. "Leave my niece alone you arms dealing asshole!" I roared. There was another collective gasp from the crowd. People were filming now—Smartphones out in droves. No doubt the scene was already Tweeted to the hilt and it wouldn't be long before it would be live on YouTube.

I heard hushed whispers of 'arms dealer,' jostling bodies gasping behind the cordoned off ropes, and VIP guests in shimmering, diaphanous gowns or crisp penguin suits, oohing and aahing; some vying for a closer view, others trying to get the hell out of our arena, and Sophie's voice screaming, "Arrete! Stop, you two."

Two hulking, balding men with earpieces suddenly came up either side of me and pulled me back. Prokovich's bodyguards. It hadn't even occurred to me to have *my* bodyguard on call. In that second, I knew what was about to happen as the Russian rose to his feet. I was going to be his punching bag while these two meatballs held my arms captive. As he came at me with a sharp left hook aimed at my gut, my leg shot higher than a Moulin Rouge can-can dancer—muscle memory kicking in (literally). I clipped him under the chin with the toe of my shoe. He flew backwards, his hand clutching his jaw in agony, blood flowing. Pearl flung herself at me, loyal to the last, screaming at Prokovich's bodyguards.

"Let my husband go, you monsters!" She was using her body

as a shield to protect me. I couldn't stop her; my arms being pinned back by the meatballs.

Elodie came rushing up, too. I expected her to shout at me but she stopped at my bleeding enemy, as he was cursing in his own language, sprawled out on the velvety red carpet. She yelled at him in French, "You ever touch my uncle again and I'll fucking *kill* you!"

I couldn't help but beam inside, a faint smile flickering on my lips. My faithful ladies with me to the bitter end. The fact that I struck first didn't matter to Elodie. *Blood is thicker than water, you Russian fuck!* My team of women, including Natalie, was screaming at the bodyguards to let me go from their beefy clutches, and soon enough, the movie theatre security arrived and the bodyguards let me free. Prokovich got back up on his feet and shook himself like a lion, his blond hair dripping with sweat; he even flashed his signature, billion-dollar smile, tinged now with scarlet blood, as our bemused audience observed us with fascination. Fitting, I thought—a bloody smile that has been bought by other people's war-zone misery.

The theatre's security team surrounded us, confused as to know what to do, asking if I was alright. They wondered if anyone wanted to press charges. They offered the same courtesy to Prokovich—but both of us pretended that our skirmish was a minor blip. As if it were a little show, put on for the crowd's entertainment. I knew I'd have to watch it from now on, though. He'd be the type to seek revenge.

Everybody straightened their ties and jackets and snickered with embarrassment, pretending, seconds later, that all was quite normal. Pearl held my hand and then Elodie also came to my side, hooking her pale, skinny arm about my elbow. She shot her lover a look, loaded with both pain and threat.

Then Pearl said coolly, "Let's go in and find our seats."

I was about to turn and walk away from the theatre but then I changed my mind. *This is Pearl's night. She has stuck by me. I'm not going anywhere.*

"Good idea, chérie, let's find our seats," I agreed, adrenaline still pumping through my gut, heating my veins. Elodie gave me a pleading look as if to say, *I'm sorry, I'll explain.* I winked at her, yet my face remained impassive. *Yes, we'll discuss this later,* it said silently—*you bet we will.* But she was still only a child in my eyes. Whoever was at fault, it wasn't Elodie. Prokovich should have known better, messing with a vulnerable teenager. He was a man of the world; she was just a fragile bird, learning to spread her wings.

There I'd been, naively assuming Elodie was a virgin. More fool me.

She couldn't have picked a bigger asshole than Mikhail Pro-kovich.

She had a lot of explaining to do.

I was so distracted that I had no idea what *Stone Trooper* was about. All I could think of was Elodie and how the fuck she ended up getting involved with the last man on Earth with whom I would have associated her. In my peripheral vision, I observed him scrutinizing her throughout the screening. He was a man obsessed. His eyes greedy, all-consuming, commanding. It was as if he wanted to swallow her whole. He was sitting on his own, though—she had spurned him as her date for the night. Why Elodie? Okay, she was beautiful and charming, but he had his pick of any supermodel. How had they become involved in the first place? I watched Elodie, her nostrils fuming like a young racehorse. I could tell that the betrayal she felt at her stepmother's cheating on her father was eating her, and whatever Prokovich had done, or not done, was making her hate him. Hate or love? The two emotions could be so intertwined.

There was a standing ovation at the end of the film. Alessandra had, no doubt, done a good job. Maybe even Oscar-worthy. Sam Myers was there in the front row, twiddling his porky fat fingers as if counting out his profits already. The movie would do well. Pearl would make a fortune. Sophie, as usual, would make a fortune. I turned to see Elodie's reaction as Alessandra took a little bow.

But Elodie was gone.

Prokovich was still there, his eyes roaming the theatre. He too, clocked her disappearance.

I whispered to Pearl, "I need to find Elodie."

"Go," she agreed. "I'll get a ride home with Sophie and Alessandra. Get out of here before you end up in another fight. I love you, even if you are a hotheaded, proud Frenchman who causes scenes."

I kissed her hand and dashed out while the audience was still clapping and cheering. As I made my exit, I passed Prokovich who was still standing, his eyes scanning the theatre. I called Elodie on my cell. No answer. But seconds later, it buzzed with a message from her:

I'm fine. Had to get out of there. C U at yours.

I'd been expecting her to run—take a flight to Paris or something. She was going to my *apartment?* I felt white heat on my face and when I looked up, I noticed a thousand cameras flashing in my face. News reporters were all over me, shoving microphones up against my lips. A woman, whom I recognized from TV said, "Mr. Chevalier, can you explain why you and Mr. Prokovich came to blows earlier this evening?"

Another reporter shouted at me, "Are either of you pressing charges? Suing for damages?"

"We're European," I answered, "so we're not into suing." Then I realized my wry joke may not have gone down too well and I wished I'd kept my trap shut.

Someone else yelled over the crowd, "Does your animosity with each other have anything to do with professional jealousy? You're both the same age. Which one of you two is richer?"

"No comment," I said briskly as I weaved my way between a sea of bodies.

I tried to hail a cab but it had started to drizzle. Barcelona and New York—two cities with a dearth of taxis the second rain threatens. I started jogging. It would be faster for me to simply run home through Central Park than mess about with either hailing a cab or calling my driver.

I needed to get to Elodie before Prokovich sent in his Rott-weilers.

16

I slipped quietly into the living room and found Elodie staring at the TV, sitting between Sally and Jeanine, all of them eating popcorn on the sofa. They were glued to the news. Rex was also watching the news, his ears cocked when he saw my face on the screen, and heard my words, "We're not into suing."

A newsroom reporter happily sang, "In a surprising turn of events, two of the wealthiest young men in the world came to blows tonight on the red carpet at a New York screening of the blockbuster movie, *Stone Trooper.* French Internet mogul, Alexandre Chevalier, and real estate magnet, Mikhail Prokovich, who hails from Russia, threw a few punches and kicks, before the HookedUp billionaire's wife, Pearl Chevalier, intervened. Apparently, the two twenty-six year old men laughed it off afterwards, Mr. Prokovich telling news reporters that they were 'just practicing a few black-belt moves as a joke.' He says that the two of them are close friends and are even discussing a future business deal together."

"Business deal, my ass," I said to the TV. "Close friends...yeah right. Don't believe what you hear, ladies."

Jeanine turned her head, and with a bewildered look on her face said, "Oh, hi Mr. Chevalier; didn't hear you come in."

"You know to call me just Alexandre, Jeanine. Are the twins asleep?"

"They were angels all evening. Didn't cry once. And yeah, they're fast asleep."

Elodie shoved a handful of popcorn into her mouth as if to prevent herself from speaking. Surely she had a lot to tell me. A whole damn lot.

"How was the movie?" Sally asked me.

"I don't know, I wasn't paying attention because something more important was distracting me. Elodie, tell them what you thought of *Stone Trooper.*"

"It sucked," she said. "Alessandra Demarr is a crap actress."

"That bad, eh? Ladies, feel free to go home; I can take it from here." I could tell they were dying to ask me questions about what happened but my stony face had both of them rise from the sofa. Elodie continued stuffing popcorn into her mouth, every now and then offering Rex some.

"I need to get going," Jeanine said with an embarrassed smile.

"Me too," Sally chimed in. "I'll be back at seven for Rex's walk tomorrow." Rex got up too, his tail spinning like a windmill, the middle of his torso wiggling with excitement. Pretty girls, sofa, popcorn, his dad on TV—what an exciting evening he'd had.

"Night, girls, and thanks so much for looking after the twins."

"Sure." Jeanine smiled awkwardly at me.

"Don't worry, Sally, I haven't forgotten our deal." An all-paid vacation in Venice, Italy, for a week. *An offer she couldn't refuse.* Sometimes, it was really fun to be so wealthy—to 'magic' people every so often. Give them treats they could never afford themselves.

The two women left, and Elodie sat cross-legged on the couch, still eating popcorn.

"So?" I said.

She arched a brow. "So."

"Aren't you going to fill me in?"

"What is there to tell?" she said in a morose, fuck-you tone.

"If you don't tell me, I'll guess and my imagination is probably wilder than reality."

"I doubt that very much," she answered enigmatically.

"How did you meet?"

"Maman and I were having lunch in Paris and he was there. He came over to our table."

"And then what?"

"He became obsessed. Started pursuing me relentlessly. Wouldn't take no for an answer."

"But he's very handsome. And rich. Girls love men like him."

"Like I really give a shit about money."

"You're a headstrong girl. You could have told him to fuck off."

She gave Rex another handful of popcorn. "I did. But he wouldn't listen. It made him want me more."

"So you started sleeping with him?"

"I don't want to discuss my sex life with *you,* you're my uncle. It's weird." She kept her eyes on the TV. *The Vampire Diaries* or something.

"He didn't seem to have a problem with blaring it out in public. It was tacky and crude what he did, telling me he was fucking you like that. In public, for everyone to hear. Even if he said it in French."

"He *is* tacky and crude. He can drink anyone under the table; he fights like a boxer." And she muttered under her breath, "He's insatiable."

"So why did you ask him as your date to the premiere?"

"I don't know."

"Are you in love with him?"

"I hate him."

I turned the sound of the TV down with the remote. "That wasn't my question. Are you in *love* with him?"

"I got hooked in."

"How long have you been seeing him for?"

"On and off."

"So that's why you asked to borrow my bodyguard a while ago?"

"Yeah."

"And why you took off traveling across America in Pearl's car?"

"I wanted to get away from him."

"But you came back to him?"

She said quietly, "I couldn't stop myself."

"Why?" she didn't answer. "Why?" I repeated.

"Because."

"Because?"

"Because I couldn't keep away from him even though I knew it was all wrong...alright? Satisfied now?"

I read between the lines. "There's more to a relationship than just sex, Elodie."

"Oh that's rich, coming from you!"

"What are you talking about?"

"You and Pearl. You're obsessed with each other. You're relationship is so physical."

She'd stabbed me in the gut with her words. "That's so not true. It started off that way. Partly. But we're soul mates. It's a feeling that can't be explained—can't be rationalized. Pearl and I were made for each other and the physical part of it just enhanced that. It's about trust. Trust made the physical bond more intense. Without trust everything else is temporary."

Elodie seemed to listen to what I said, mulling my words of wisdom over in her mind. She then told me, "I came here so I'd be safe from Mikhail. I can't go back to my apartment in the Village."

"You did the right thing. Stay here. Stay as long as you like—you can even help us look after the twins."

"He'll be out there waiting for me. Obsessing about me. He won't rest until he has me. All of me. He told me so."

I knew this sort of stuff was an aphrodisiac for many women. My mother had succumbed to those sorts of promises with my father. Abuse dressed up as love and passion when, really, it was all about control. Hell, my mom's fictional boyfriends were probably full of that kind of talk. I feared that Elodie would be

swayed by Prokovich's amour, even if it was more about posses-
sion than real love. "Well, you'll just need protection, plus a
strong will to keep away from him."

"I *mean* it this time. I don't want him in my life. He's not a
good person."

"How do you know he's not a good person?" *I know, but how
does she know?*

"I've heard him make deals on the phone. I know who he is."

"He doesn't worry about you being party to all that?"

"No. He likes it. It makes him feel powerful. He wants me to
fear him."

"And *do* you fear him?" I asked.

"D'you know why I decided I didn't want to see him anymore? Why I couldn't love him?"

"I can think of a million reasons not to love a man who
makes his money selling arms," I said, taking in her little heart-
shaped face and her innocent gaze, which was breaking me up.

"Governments do it," she said by way of an excuse. "He's no
worse than a lot of politicians."

"I know, Elodie. We live in a pretty fucked up world. But you
deserve better than a man like that. What was it then, that finally
made you decide you didn't love him?"

"He told me he strangled a cat when he was a boy. I felt sick
when he said that." She blew air from her lips and added, "I wish
he'd get blown up by one of his own land mines. Or someone
would fucking shoot him with one of his AK-47s."

I fixed my eyes on her wide brown eyes. "Don't do anything
rash. You hear me? Just keep away from him."

"Hey guys, you all look very serious." It was Pearl, swishing back from the premiere in her heels and shimmery gown. Rex bounded over to her but luckily didn't jump up. "Glad you're here, Elodie," Pearl said. "Anyone for a snack? I'm starving."

"You relax, chérie, I'll check on the twins and make us some sandwiches or something."

"I already took a peep. They're out for the count; Louis has a little grin on his face and Madeleine's pouting in her sleep, dreaming about something serious."

I left Pearl and Elodie together and snuck into the babes' room and observed them in their cots. It was true what Pearl said about their little expressions. We'd been lucky; neither of them were screamers. Sometimes babies come into a world with everything just right. Others have a battle. I was one of the battle fighters. I'd had colic, apparently. Then whooping cough—I had a rough ride. But Louis and Madeleine had two parents madly in love with each other and seemed to be living a stress-free exist-ence. It showed in their faces and in their jolly demeanor.

As I slipped out noiselessly and walked past the living room, I couldn't help but hear a snippet of Elodie and Pearl's hushed conversation.

"He became more and more dominant, you know. He made me play games with whips and stuff. Tied me up. Blinded me."

"Blindfolded you, you mean?" Pearl corrected.

I did that to Pearl, even though all I did was 'whip' her with a feather. But still. Shit, maybe I'm just as fucked up as Prokovich.

"Yeah," Elodie went on. "You know, at first it was…well, it was kind of fascinating and I wanted to please him. But it got more and more crazy. Then I left him and he promised he'd stop but when we started dating again, he wanted to do the kinky stuff and I got scared."

"You mustn't see him if he scares you, sweetie," Pearl advised her.

"He told me that we're meant to be together, that he can't live without me. That I'm his life, his breath, his moon and stars."

"Fancy words coming from such a tough man."

"He's crazy about me."

"*Crazy* sounds like a good word to describe him. You're in love?" Pearl asked.

I moved on to the kitchen. I didn't want to intrude anymore. I fixed us all some sandwiches and drinks but as I came back towards the living room with the tray, I heard more. I stopped in my tracks.

"You know, each time I cut myself, it makes me feel better. Like a relief."

"You need to see someone about this, Elodie. You could wind up bleeding to death."

"I stopped. I'd stopped for ages."

"But you started again?" Pearl asked softly.

"Just that one time."

"Honey, you need to stay here with us. Sort yourself out. See a therapist, you know; we need to find you a professional to talk to."

I stood there, wanting to come in but I was hesitant about interrupting their heartfelt conversation. If I budged, they'd know I was there. I remained motionless, hoping they'd move onto another topic and I could make my entrance. Then I missed a bit as they were talking in such quiet voices. Then Pearl asked:

"So you told your mom about the rape?"

"No, never."

"Why not?"

"Because I was so young—I thought if I didn't talk about it, it would go away."

Pearl's tone was gentle but ominous. "It never goes away, not even if you have amnesia."

That's when I came into the room. "Who's got amnesia?" I said lightheartedly. "Rex? Forgotten he's already had a load of popcorn and is now after our sandwiches?"

"Thanks, honey," Pearl said, helping me unload the tray. "I could eat...I was about to say 'a horse' but I guess with the French eating horses, that isn't such a great expression."

"Yeah, yeah, yeah," I sang. "Very funny. I'll have you know the other day, in some 'health food' takeout restaurant, somewhere near Washington Square, they were serving up kangaroo meat, so it's not just the French."

"That's gross." Elodie winced.

"We should all be like Leonardo da Vinci," I said. "All be full-on vegetarians, then we could feel blameless."

"Apparently lettuces scream when you pull them up," Elodie told us, but then she shifted her eyes mournfully to the Jim Dine painting on the wall that I'd given Pearl for her engagement gift: the multi-colored heart. Elodie's look said, *I wish I could find that kind of love.* "I'm going to bed. Let you two love birds be in peace."

"Don't you want a sandwich?" I asked.

"No, I'm good. And it's so late. So Parisian, to eat at this hour. Night. See you in the morning."

"Night, sweetie. We'll talk some more tomorrow." Pearl blew

her a kiss and sank back into the sofa. She tucked her legs under her, and spread out her beautiful chiffon dress.

We delved into the sandwiches. Five minutes later, I couldn't contain my curiosity any longer. "I know it was a private girls' talk but I did overhear a bit of your conversation."

Pearl shook her head. "Eavesdropper."

"I know. I'm sorry. But I *worry* about my niece; I want to help her. If I'd known what her problems were, perhaps she wouldn't have fallen into the arms of the wrong man in the first place."

"She's young and impressionable. Mikhail Prokovich is handsome, rich, charming. He dates supermodels. And he made a beeline for her. She must have been very flattered; very swept off her feet. It's not surprising she fell for him."

I bit into a corner of my cheese sandwich and realized that cheese wasn't the best choice so late at night. Perhaps we'd be awake for hours. "I heard the word 'rape,'" I admitted.

"Elodie told me that in *confidence*, Alexandre."

"I still overheard. What happened? And when?"

Pearl dabbed her lips with a napkin, rested her hands on her mouth as if considering whether she should divulge another person's secret. I looked at her expectantly. Then she sighed and finally said, "It was her best friend's older brother. She thought it was her first kiss but he went further and forced her to have sex with him. She'd had a crush on him for years and was crazy about him, but in an innocent, sweet way. But he took her against her will. Apparently, he was a real brute about it. She was only fourteen. He was much older—nineteen. Worse, he wanted nothing to do with her afterwards and her best friend abandoned her, so she felt totally betrayed all round."

I scrunched up my brow. "Six degrees of separation. But from rape of some kind. It amazes me how many people have been affected directly, or indirectly, by abuse. Join the fucking club. Poor thing. About the same time she started dressing like a Goth and wearing spiky heels."

"Exactly. Her defense mechanism."

"I also heard the word 'cut,' " I said.

Pearl grimaced. "Unfortunately, she's a cutter."

"You sound like you're familiar with that term."

"My brother, John...you know, he also cut himself. Sadly, it's quite common."

I screwed up my face, imagining a slicing razor blade. "Ouch."

"Elodie's thing is words. I noticed a scar on her stomach a few weeks ago and tonight I asked her about it. It seemed the right moment as she was confiding in me."

"What do you mean, *her thing is words?*"

"She carves words into her flesh. She cut the word JAMAIS into her hip."

"The word 'never'. Never what?"

"She said it made her feel better. And in control."

I raked my hands through my hair. "Jesus. Poor girl. She needs to see a shrink or a therapist."

"She says she *is* already seeing someone."

I let out a lungful of air which I didn't realize I'd been holding in. "Is this what we're in for, for the next twenty years? Fucked-up kids who carve themselves and end up playing bondage games with ruthless arms dealers? Maybe becoming parents was a bad idea, Pearl."

"Oh, so I guess you heard that part of our talk too?" Pearl raised her brows. "You caught that part of our *private* conversation? About the kinky stuff?"

"I told you when we met, I think girls Elodie's age are too young to get wrapped up in sexual games like that. Yes, I heard your conversation. I have ears like Rex—sorry but I can't help it. *La Legion* made me that way. I hear everything. See everything, whether I like it or not."

"You're right about her being impressionable—she said she was playing along to please him but he got out of control. And that she became scared of him."

"He better stay the fuck away from her."

"And what if she doesn't want him to? She's an adult; we can't control her life. She has to choose for herself, Alexandre."

"I'll talk to her again tomorrow," I said.

17

But I didn't get a chance to talk to Elodie the following day because she disappeared before I'd even gotten out of bed. She left her phone behind so I couldn't call her. I stood in the spare room—Elodie's clothing and make-up scattered all over the floor. I had no idea where she had gone. Out for breakfast? Would she be back any moment? I was contemplating contacting Sophie but my sister got there first. I answered my cell.

"What the fuck," Sophie began, her voice a pack of ice.

I knew what she was referring to. I couldn't resist an, *I told you so.* "Well, if you hadn't been so gung-ho about having meetings with that shifty bastard in the first place—"

"Yeah, yeah, it's all my fault. And now Elodie hates me because of Alessandra."

"You should have talked to her a long time ago about all that. What did you expect? Elodie's an adult now; she had a right to know. You betrayed her by not trusting her and keeping her in the dark. So yes, you've got a lot of work ahead of you to repair the damage."

Sophie groaned into the receiver. "Thanks for the vote of confidence, dear brother."

"Sophie, you need to come out of the closet. It's not fair on anybody, least of all Elodie. Not to mention your poor longsuffering husband."

" 'Poor, longsuffering husband' has been having affairs for years. Neither of us asks the other any questions; we lead separate lives."

"Fine, but Elodie shouldn't be piggy in the middle."

"Where is she? She won't answer her phone and I want to talk to her. She told me last night she'd be staying with you. I was thinking of coming over but thought I should call first."

"She's not here. She's upset. Upset with you, upset with having got involved with Prokovich, upset with shit that went down in her past."

"What shit?"

"That's for her to tell. It's not my place."

"She's been confiding in you and not me?" Sophie's voice cracked—it sounded as if the floodgates were about to open.

"Not exactly. Look, I'm not going to discuss Elodie's private affairs with you. Ask her yourself," I said.

Sophie gave out a loud sigh. "She told me she didn't want anything to *do* with me."

"She'll come around—just give it time. Look, I've got to go. I can hear the babies waking up."

"Wow, you're taking fatherhood so seriously."

"You bet. I want to be the father I never had myself."

"Talk to Elodie for me, will you. Please get her to call me."

"I'll try my best."

"Anyway," I said later, in an angry rush, while Pearl and I were up on the roof terrace having lunch in the conservatory—my eyes fixed on Pearl as if it were all her fault. "What the fuck happened with your documentary on exposing arms dealers? You even had dinner with the bastard, why haven't you told the world what an asshole he is already?"

"I wish it were that easy," Pearl replied calmly, deflecting my rage with a flick of her wrist.

"Well what's the fucking problem? His name is all over the news now. He and I are more notorious than ever. Grab him while you can!"

"He's a slippery fish, Mikhail Prokovich—you know that. There's no proof, as such. You can't go around accusing someone of something *that major* until you have the guilty package all wrapped up with a nice big bow. The more famous they are, the more delicate the situation."

"Well hurry up about it, baby; I'm losing patience."

"Oh, we're working on it, believe me. The research is complicated. *He* is complicated. Clever. It's hard to link him directly to any shady dealings. If we attack at this point, we could lose everything—all our hard work up till now. We need to be patient. Plus, he's connected to governments and big businesses. We're in cahoots with 60 Minutes and the BBC's Panorama, because we need clout. HookedUp Enterprises can't do this alone. We could get our asses sued if we aren't careful. And despite your little quip about Europeans not suing, I'm sure we'd have Prokovich's lawyers jumping down our throats, crawling all over us, the second they could."

My fists were clenched in tight balls while Pearl coolly sliced a piece of homemade quiche for us both and served us each a small portion of green salad. She carefully poured us each a glass of Pinot Grigio, the crisp white wine—as chilled as she was.

I had married a headstrong woman who complimented my character in every way. She wasn't riled by things when it came to her career. It seemed she had everything managed, including me. Her presence calmed me.

I had certainly chosen the perfect woman to be my wife.

"Anyway," I concluded, "that fuck has some heavy karma coming his way. By hook or by crook, he'll pay for being such an asshole."

Pearl started laughing.

"What's so funny? Are you laughing at my accent, Mrs. Chevalier? The fact that I don't pronounce the H?"

"Not your accent but I love it when you use expressions like 'by hook or by crook.' Do we even know where that comes from? Crook, as in crooked? Hook, as in a shepherd's hook or something?"

"It's probably derived from some obscure village in England called Crook or Hook. Anyway, right now, my focus is on Elodie. I'm worried about her. Obviously she left her cell phone behind on purpose so I can't find her."

Pearl frowned. "That means you can't track her down with

the GPS, right? The way you did with me."

"Thanks for that, you make me sound like a real stalker."

She winked at me. "Well you are, Alexandre Chevalier. You stalked me all the way to the alter."

I 'crooked' my finger at her and patted my lap. "Come here, you sexy wife, sit on my knee. Where are the twins?"

"Having their nap. I've got the baby monitor on. Modern spyware. See?" She showed me her Smartphone. "Sleeping like angels."

"Where's Rex?"

"In the park with Sally."

"Patricia and the staff?"

"It's her day off. The rest of the staff left for the afternoon."

"So we're alone?"

Pearl looked at her Reverso watch—a gift from me. "Maybe for an hour or so more."

"Fuck lunch—it's you I want to eat," I said, lust glittering in my eyes, not breaking my gaze from hers. "You looked so beautiful last night, chérie, in your elegant gown. And I can still smell whatever you put on. Or maybe it's just your natural scent. Whatever your secret is, it has me intoxicated. Get your ass over here."

Pearl smiled and swept her hand over her golden locks, pushing her hair away from her face. She got up and sat on my knee. I was instantly hard. Fuck, even after giving birth and all the intricacies that came with child rearing and a household to run, she had me on red alert. She nuzzled her butt into my groin subtly and I could hear a throaty growl which surprised me as my own. I burrowed my nose into her elegant neck and smelled the

Pearl Elixir that had me permanently mesmerized.

I kissed the nape of her soft neck. "Do you remember when we had our first bath together? I read you poetry and you slipped in the oily lavender water and the book flipped out of my hands and sank?"

"I most certainly do," she said. "I thought I'd spoiled the moment but you laughed—your first edition Baudelaire ruined."

I nipped her lobe and she shuddered. I saw goose bumps rise on her flesh. "And then we discussed the power," I whispered in her ear, "of smell and how two people can be attracted to each other for no other reason than pheromones?" I inhaled her sweet essence and a rush of desire surged through my torso, hammering in my groin.

"And I wondered if it was the lavender oil alone which had me hooked on you."

"I'd never felt so at ease with a woman before. I'd never had that intimacy before," I murmured.

Pearl sounded surprised. "Really?"

"Really," I said, my hand cupping her succulent ass. "You know when you're listening to an old vinyl record and it jams? That was my life before. In a rut. And when you came along, the needle jumped forward into the right groove and forced me to move ahead. Finally I could hear the melody—it flowed beautifully, and I knew the way it was meant to sound."

She turned her head and smiled. "I'm a melody? I'm music to your ears?"

I gripped her thigh. "The best melody ever. You have the perfect beat, Pearl, the perfect rhythm. You soothe me. You enliven me. You make me dance. You help me sleep. Yes, you're my music, chérie." I sneaked my fingers between her legs and felt her moistness through the thin fabric of her panties. The fact that I caused such an instant physical reaction in her body made my cock ache with need. We hadn't fucked for nearly a week—that's what having children did—and it felt like a lifetime. I lifted her sweater and snaked my other hand around her smooth waist. "How do you keep so fit? So trim?"

"Trade secret," she answered, nestling her butt into my solid, pounding erection. I spun her around and moved her soft thighs either side of my legs so she was straddling me. I cupped her chin with my hand and pulled her beautiful face towards mine. I didn't kiss her straight away. I wanted to look into her eyes and really *see* her. Those guileless, big blue eyes that could have belonged to a little girl. I breathed her in.

"You're sniffing me again, aren't you?" she teased, her arms closing tightly around my shoulders. "You're worse than Rex."

"Caught me," I said with a laugh.

"What do I smell of?"

"Of Pearl."

"What *is* Pearl?"

"It's unique. The pure essence of love. A secret potion. There's no smell like it in the world—it's deep and nuanced and...fresh. With a hint of sunshine. It makes my head spin every time. If I could bottle it, it would earn me more money than all of my enterprises combined. But then again, I wouldn't want to share your elixir with anybody."

I rested my lips on her mouth, my breath a tease, and with the tip of my tongue explored her Cupid's bow. Such a pretty mouth, that belonged to a woman of another era, like one of

Rossetti's Pre-Raphaelites. My hand, still on her jaw, slowly traced down her neck to her shoulder. And then to the curve of her breast. She gasped. I could feel her hardened nipple through the delicate cashmere of her sweater. I trailed more light kisses around her mouth, stroking my tongue across her bottom lip and she moaned, edging her crotch up against me, and her hands moved to unbutton my jeans—my rock-hard cock, pounding with desire, sprang up against my abdomen. Fuck I felt horny.

She couldn't take my tormenting kisses any longer—her lips parted and her tongue flicked out to touch mine as she held my thick erection in her grip. Chills ran through my body at her carnal touch.

I licked into her mouth and, gripping her hair, tilted her head back. "You're mine, baby," I growled—my sound vibrating in her mouth as she played with the tip of my crown, smoothing the pre-cum around my swollen dick—as massive as a cobra. I felt like I was about to explode the kiss was so erotic, and I couldn't wait to enter her. But this foreplay was too beautiful to rush. We were fucking each other with our mouths, our tongues in a wild, wet tango, nipping, biting, stroking, rimming. I kept hold of her hair, not letting her go; my possessive nature a fire, stoked by her love for me.

"Your kisses are my food," Pearl whimpered into my mouth as I consumed her whole. And it was true; we were nourishment for each other. It was as if I were eating her with my lashing tongue—sucking her, tasting her essence. Feasting on the Pearl Elixir.

I needed her so much.

"Sit on my cock, baby," I murmured. "Slide yourself onto

me." My hands moved down to her ass which I grasped voraciously—my emotions and desire in a frenzy. I heard a cry, timorous and panicked—for a second, I thought it was Pearl.

She shifted herself away from me and leaned down to grab her cell. "It's Louis," she told me, staring at the screen of her Smartphone. He never yelled that way—I could see why she jumped to attention. "I'd better go downstairs and see if he's okay."

"I'll come with you." I let out a sigh. Fatherhood. A full-time job.

Pearl took Louis to the pediatrician, and I stayed behind with Madeleine, just in case what he had was contagious—two sick babies wouldn't be the greatest, although it was the first time they had ever been separated and I felt badly for them. I coddled her in my arms, rocking her gently. I put on a Vivaldi cello concerto and swayed with her about the apartment, which made her coo and smile—her toothless grin a joy to behold, which sent a rush of butterflies, circling my stomach. I nestled my face against her pearly, soft skin—she too exuded a secret elixir: the baby elixir that was almost as intoxicating as Pearl's.

I kept my eye on my cell, hoping that Elodie would call any second. My instinct told me that she'd be alright. But there was nothing I could do for now. She'd told me she wouldn't be going to her apartment in the Village, but I called her roommate anyway. Nothing.

Women always complain about how tough it is to be female

but shit, in that moment, I was in turmoil. Worried about Elodie, my twins, my belle Pearl. Feeling an overwhelming urge to protect them all, but not knowing how.

A few hours later, Pearl and Louis were back home from the doctor—what he was ailing from was just a very bad cold. I felt a huge sense of gratitude. I realized that this was to be a constant feature in our lives as parents: nerves on the edge with worry. And I needed to develop a more *laissez-faire* attitude about my kids or I'd drive myself, and everyone around me, nuts.

But just as Louis had finally settled and was completely calm, and I was finally enjoying a beer, my cell went. It was Elodie. At last. It was well after midnight.

Elodie asked me to meet her. She told me that she was in a brownstone on the Upper East Side and gave me the address; but then we got cut off. I knew the building well because I'd thought about buying it once, when it was up for sale. Obviously someone outbid me. Outbid *me!* Whoever it was, had stupid money. Prokovich himself? Surely not. Elodie said she wanted to stay clear of him and he'd hardly be inviting me over to his house. I imagined it must belong to the parents of one of her friend's, and that they were away for the weekend.

I exited the delivery door of my apartment building, just in case any paparazzi were waiting to take a snap at me out front. Fuck, I hated being newsworthy. As I waited for my driver a block away, I wondered what I was going to do about my niece. It dawned on me that, although I had always envisioned her as so innocent, she was a wild card. But still a damaged bird. Those bloody damaged birds—Pearl included—that had me running around after them, trying to fix their wings, when they were probably perfectly capable of looking after themselves.

I thought of Pearl and our unfinished business at lunch. I had her on top of me in my mind's eye, or my cock in her luscious mouth—her big blue, childlike eyes looking up at me. Like a child with a tasty lollipop. Damn. Images of her sucking me off kept flitting through my one-track mind—it was on replay. I knew now what it must be like to be fat and on a diet, constantly craving treats you can't have. I wanted Pearl at all times, but lately, something always intervened. Namely: kids.

And now, Elodie.

My cell buzzed. It was Elodie again. "Where are you?" I said urgently. "I mean I know where you are—I'm on my way—but whose place is it?"

"In someone's house."

"Obviously, but whose?"

"I'm in trouble. Bad. Really bad."

"Stay where you are, I'm on my way, I won't be long," I promised.

"There's blood everywhere," she whispered.

"Blood? Jesus, what happened? Are you hurt?"

"I'm fine. It's him. He's hurt."

"Okay, stay calm. Who's 'him'?" I knew who *him* was but I wanted to hear it from her lips.

Silence.

"Elodie, who is him?"

"He's lying in a pool of blood."

"Is anyone trying to hurt you? Can he hurt you? Is anyone else there?" I whispered hoarsely into the line.

"I think he's dead." She sounded unfazed. Very matter-of-fact.

"How much blood?"

"He's in the bathtub."

"Did you bind the wound? Get a shirt, or something, and tie it tight about the wound. He might just be injured; did you check his pulse? Elodie, are you listening to me?"

"It's too late for that now."

"Jesus," I said, my heart pounding with blood-soaked images in my head. What had she done? Attacked him with her killer heels? Although with Elodie being so tiny, I couldn't imagine her getting very far. "Who knows you're there?"

"Nobody. I've locked the front door. There's no doorman here or anyone. Nobody. I didn't do anything wrong but please don't tell Mom."

"Of that you have my word. Elodie, stay where you are. Do not open the door to anyone, is that clear? I'll be there ASAP. Do not let anyone in that house."

"I won't."

If I'd been an upright citizen I would have gotten Elodie to call 911, or call them myself. But who knew what mess she'd gotten into? I couldn't risk it. Better Prokovich dead from bleeding than Elodie in some American women's penitentiary with big butch dykes fighting over whose bunk she'd be sleeping in at night.

I called Suresh, my driver, and cancelled him, and hailed a cab instead. There was only one person I could trust with this. He was not dissimilar to the actor, Joe Pesci. Just as nuts as him—or at least the roles he plays. Small. Aggressive. Touchy. Chip on his shoulder type of guy. My man was a 'cleaner,' trained in forensics. He could make traces of blood, fingerprints, clothes fibers, et cetera...vanish. Make the body, *itself,* vanish, if need be, and if he wasn't available, he had someone who was. I called. He answered on the second ring. He was obviously used to emergencies. Strike that. His work, his trade *was* emergencies and emergencies only. Death. Blood. Emergencies of every kind. Sophie had used him once. I needed him on standby, just in case Elodie had incriminated herself. I told him to wait for my call when I knew more.

The New York traffic was full of sirens, as usual, pulsing and frenetic. People crossing the road, buying flowers from corner shops, couples arguing on the sidewalk, people walking their dogs. Saturday night, New York—a city that never sleeps.

I jumped into a cab and tried to make the driver understand where I was going. He'd been in New York for only two days and hardly spoke English. He was from Pakistan. Normally, I would have given him an interview on the spot, asked him a million questions about his country's state of affairs from his bird's eye view, his religion, and what was really going on out there—things we didn't hear about on the news. But I didn't want him remembering me, remembering my face and my destination. Just in case. Who knew what awaited me, and what shit I was going to have to clean up, courtesy of Elodie. What I did know was that trouble was on the horizon—I just hadn't added blood and guts into the equation.

I got the driver to drop me off a block away and I dashed into an all-night shop to buy a hoodie. There were none for sale so I grabbed a plastic rain poncho and a baseball cap. I put them on, once I was out of the store. With me being on the news for the last twenty-four hours, I couldn't be too careful. I imagined Mr. Square-Jaw probably had a state-of-the-art surveillance system surrounding his property.

As I climbed the steps to the brownstone, I kept my head down. What a fuck-up. I suppose I wasn't really thinking straight: I just wanted to get Elodie out of there. She came to the door. Heels off. No make-up and wearing a floaty silk dress. She looked like an angel. Except, she had bright green washing-up gloves on. Had she been watching too much CSI? She opened the door gingerly and I stepped into a very monochrome, but chic, bachelor pad hallway. The lights were off, save a faint glow coming from upstairs.

"Who's seen you here?" I whispered with urgency.

"Nobody." She looked me, and my mad attire, up and down. "His cameras are switched off, don't worry."

"How do you know?"

"Because he always disables them when he's, you know—"

"No, I don't know, Elodie. What the fuck's going on?"

She looked down, ashamed.

"Where is he?"

"Follow me. He's up here."

She led me upstairs to a bedroom. It was huge. Dark red walls, sleek, antique Asian furniture. The blinds were all drawn, but a small light in one corner cast a beam across the room. My eyes scanned the bedroom. Prokovich was not lying in a bath, at all, nor was there any blood. He was on his bed, spread out. Naked, except for two bound silk scarves noosed about his neck, hooked up to bedposts either side. There were burgundy-colored blotches about his neck; he'd been strangulated by the scarves. He had globs of dried cum around his hand and genitals. He'd been masturbating, obviously. I turned my eyes away from his private parts, but bent down to take his pulse, just to double-check. He wasn't breathing. Dead. I looked up and stared at my niece.

"I told you there was blood because I thought it was the only thing that would make you come here," she told me sheepishly. "It sounded more urgent."

"Of course I would have come, silly—you didn't have to make that up."

"I'm sorry, I—"

"And the bath?" I asked, wondering what insane part of her imagination conjured up that particular image of him, lying bleeding in a bath.

"I thought you'd be relieved. No mess."

I had to remind myself that Elodie was still a teenager. I tried to stay levelheaded, not lose my cool. I drew in a lungful of air. "Let's begin at the beginning, shall we?" I sounded like one of those nursery-rhyme readers on the radio that I listened to when I was a child. *Let's begin at the beginning.*

Elodie bit her lip and said nothing.

"I need to make a decision, goddamn it, Elodie. There's a dead man here and I have to know what the fuck's going on! Did you do this?"

"He did it to himself."

"He rigged all this up, *himself?*"

She flushed and looked down at the floor. "I helped him. He

wanted it tighter."

"So you planned all this?"

She raised her eyes and looked me in the eye, defiantly. "It was the only way I knew to get him out of my life for good."

"So you played along, pretending you were up for it?" She nodded. I knew what had happened. Apparently, cutting the oxygen supply off to the brain during orgasm causes heightened pleasure, a sort of hallucinatory ecstasy. I had read somewhere that between five hundred and a thousand deaths occur each year in the US, alone, from autoerotic asphyxiation gone wrong. *So this was the shit Prokovich was into and had Elodie running from him.*

Her mouth twisted in disgust. "I hated his sick games. But then, I was also hooked in. Is that wrong? All I wanted was to get away from him. But he kept luring me back. I thought if he was dead, he'd leave me alone, once and for all. Stop stalking me. Leave me in peace."

"So you *did* do this? Was this your idea?"

Tears were falling silently down her milk-white cheeks. She nodded.

Clever girl, I wanted to say, *A+ for imagination.* "And he was up for it?" I asked.

"He thought it was the best idea he'd ever heard."

"Where did you learn to tie that sailor's knot?"

"Remember when we went sailing once with Laura?"

"But that was years ago."

Elodie closed her lids and shook her head. "I never forgot that knot she taught me."

"And then what happened, after you helped him tie himself up?"

"I put some music on. Turned down the lights, lit a scented candle, got him in the mood. Got him going, you know, till he was really into it. Played along; did a striptease. Then I left just as....you know. I went downstairs and poured myself a glass of wine. I did some washing-up to distract myself. When I came back...I didn't expect that it would have actually worked. I thought he'd stop, that he'd..."

I inspected the tight sailor's knot and the whole crazy set-up, but making sure I didn't touch anything. It was obvious that the guy had had an accomplice, or someone who'd helped get him into that position. The last thing I wanted was Elodie implicated in this dirty scandal and one of his Russian aides swooping down on her in revenge. Or, worse, some psycho ex girlfriend, or current girlfriend—the guy fucked around—plotting retribution.

"Did any neighbors hear anything? Did he make a noise?"

"They're all away for the weekend in The Hamptons."

"How do you know?"

"Because he told me. He said he loved staying in New York when everyone else was out of town because it was quieter."

I dialed Joe Pesci's doppelganger. He'd need to make it look as if the Russian had done all this alone; an accidental, autoerotic 'suicide.' He'd need to wipe the whole place down for prints, hairs, anything incriminating. I spoke quietly into my cell, giving him instructions and the address, telling him I'd leave the front door off the latch, not that that would have been a problem; the guy could pick any lock. I pressed end.

"Pin your hair back, Elodie. Get a hat or a scarf out of his closet and hide your hair. Here, use this," I said, fishing a silk handkerchief out of my jacket. "Don't put anymore washing-up glove fingerprints anywhere. You'll need a hat to hide your face. We're going to walk out of here with our heads down and hope to hell that nobody saw you come in. What time did you arrive?"

"A few hours ago."

"So when did he….pass out, exactly?"

"I killed him, didn't I?" she said, her lips twitching with re-morse.

"No, Elodie, you did not." I held her by the shoulders. "Get this into your head: You. Are. Not. Responsible. For this son of a bitch's downfall. He had it fucking coming to him. Is that clear?"

"But I helped, it was my—"

"No buts. All you did was speed up the inevitable. Help him do to himself what Karma had planned for him all along. This bastard was responsible for millions of innocent citizens' deaths all over the world. You did the world a favor by helping him reach Hell a little faster."

"Please don't tell anyone. Don't tell Maman."

"Come on, let's get out of here." I peeled the rubber gloves off her delicate hands, rolled them into a ball and put them inside my jacket pocket. I held her hands. "Elodie, you and I are peas in a pod. We both have a darkness that lives inside us. And that's okay. I've been responsible for a few deaths, myself. I'm *here* for you. Always and forever. I understand you. What you did *had* to be done. This is *our* secret, no one else's. I swear, I won't tell a soul. Not even Pearl—who'll be delighted, by the way, when she reads in the papers that this bastard has snuffed it." I drew my niece to me, my arms tight about her tiny frame, and let her sob against my chest.

18

Elodie left the country two days later. Our choice of destination was South America. She'd been clamoring to go backpacking for ages and this was her chance. Art school could wait. We needed for her to lie low for a good six months.

The news was full of Prokovich. Just as I suspected, one of his girlfriends discovered his body the following day. Luckily, nobody mentioned Elodie. Not seriously, anyway. One reporter did call, asking why they were chatting together at the *Stone Trooper* premiere and I said she'd met him once with her mother. I was worried I'd be a suspect in people's eyes after our skirmish on the red carpet, but my man had done such a thorough job in Prokovich's brownstone, that forensics had unequivocal 'suicide' as the cause of death. Sophie had a contact at the NYPD who filled her in. We were free and clear. Elodie was safe. Still, I didn't want her in New York, just in case she let something slip. I encouraged her go backpacking like a hippy. She'd be far, far away from a world of red carpets, bondage and billionaires. She could go surfing along the coast of Peru and Ecuador, eat *ceviche* and study *The Lonely Planet*. Maybe find herself a nice, simple surfer boyfriend who cared about waves and a nice cold beer at the end of the day, not some fucked up control freak, world-playing megalomaniac who'd once strangled animals to death and had no respect for human life. Elodie needed a salt-of-the-earth type. Armed with a Smartphone, she'd be fine. And I realized now that she didn't need looking after. Not one bit.

She was an enigma. Dark like me. Luc Besson's *La Femme Nikita*. They recruited women like Elodie—she had what it took to be a mercenary. She had a ruthless streak. Intelligent. Savvy. She was a schemer, a planner, a loner by nature. She'd be alright, I decided.

Life went on uneventfully, except that Pearl was working very hard with HookedUp Enterprises and Rex got married to a stunning black Labrador who gave birth to six glorious, silky black pups. We took a house for the month of February in The Bahamas, and Pearl managed to do business from her laptop on the beach. The Smartphone was used minimally—why? Because she was pregnant again! Five months and counting. I hadn't even imagined we'd be blessed again with another pregnancy.

We were lying on the beach, the waves lapping gently—a pale turquoise water shimmering and glittering us with its welcome. The sand was almost white and squeaked beneath our feet. Pearl lay under an umbrella, and Louis and Madeleine were happily playing. A new nanny (Sally had her hands full with all the dogs, who were in New York—too hot here for them) had come with us so we didn't have to worry about having eyes in the back of our heads.

"What are you laughing at?" I asked Pearl. She was stretched out on her towel, reading *Vanity Fair*. HookedUp Enterprises had just bought the magazine.

"This interview they did with you in Paris. You're such a liar!"

I narrowed my eyes. "Which bit are you reading?"

"You told them we were living in a tree-house in Thailand."

"I like my anonymity, you know that. Let them send their paparazzi out to Thailand and leave us alone peacefully here. What else does it say?" I asked, looking up at a cloudless blue sky.

"I'll read it out loud and you can hear for yourself what a bull-shitter you are."

"Go on then, I'm all ears."

"INTERVIEW WITH ALEXANDRE CHEVALIER FOR VANITY FAIR. By Stacey Black," Pearl began.

'It's 4pm and I'm waiting nervously in the lobby of the George V in Paris to meet one of the top five richest men in the world. That, in itself, is impressive enough, espe-

cially considering this man is a renowned philanthropist and gives a percentage of his income to charity. But the fact that he is only twenty-six years old and looks like a movie star makes most people quiver at the knees, including myself. His name? None other than Alexandre Chevalier, CEO of the billion-dollar Internet phenomenon, HookedUp, bigger than Twitter and Facebook and with an offer on the table from Google, poised for a historical buyout that is bigger than most nations' national yearly budgets.'

"Sounds like this Stacey Black has a major crush on you, darling," Pearl teased.

I grinned. I couldn't deny I liked keeping Pearl on her toes. "Read on, this is interesting."

'Finally, Monsieur Chevalier saunters into the lobby. He is wearing dark glasses – very Hollywood. My stomach flips. I shouldn't be so in awe. But I am. This man is power personified. He is dressed in a sharp, obviously hand-tailored, charcoal-gray suit, contrary to how he is usually described; favoring T-shirt and jeans, even for business meetings. I stand up and he smiles at me. Sadly, the smile is kept in check. This is a married man, after all. A man famously in love with his wife. He shakes my hand in a professional manner and takes off his shades. Two searing green eyes greet me. Alexandre Chevalier is devastatingly handsome. But enough of that...I'm here to do an interview.'

"Yes, she definitely had the hots for you, Alexandre."
"Read on, chérie."

'A.C. Sorry I'm late. I got held up.

V.F. It's so great to meet you and thank you for doing this exclusive interview.

A.C. You're welcome. Shall we go through to the restaurant or bar? We can have some tea or something. I lived in London for a while so I picked up a few British habits. Nothing like an afternoon cup of tea to get the brain back on track.

Brain back on track? I doubt it. As well as being an astute businessman, Alexandre Chevalier is known for his brilliance. Self-educated, he started HookedUp with his sister, Sophie Dumas, with no more than 15,000 Euros— a loan from their stepfather. It wasn't long before this French sibling team took the social media world by storm.

We sit down and are presented with a menu. I ask him to choose. My French is not up to much. Besides, hearing him speak his native language is a treat indeed. A waiter comes up to our table and hovers there reverently. Everybody knows who Alexandre Chevalier is, it seems. He orders us Lapsang Souchong tea and some petits fours. I start with my questions.

V.F. Is it true, Mr. Chevalier, that you're retiring?

A.C. (He laughs.) Probably for a nanosecond, and then I'll stick my fingers into some other pie. I am selling HookedUp. Rather, my sister and I are selling. By the way, call me Alexandre—I hate formalities.

V.F. Is it true that you have been offered ten billion dollars for your company?

A.C. I never discuss money unless it's with my accountant or lawyer. *(He narrows his eyes at me.)*

V.F. Okay, well, there is something else that people are dying to know. Rex, your dog, has become a household name since you and your family were all photographed in Central Park together by the paparazzi. Is it true that your dog has become a father?

A.C. Yes, his wife/girlfriend, whatever, has just given birth. I'm glad to say that she's had six very healthy puppies. *(A trace of a smile makes it evident that he is amused by my question.)*

V.F. And is it also true that Rex gave his lady-dog a diamond collar that is worth hundreds of thousands of dollars?

A.C. *(He laughs.)* Never believe what you read.

Pearl stopped reading and burst out laughing. "Sally bought that for Bonnie. It was a cheapie thing from one of those accessory stores. So funny. Sorry, I'll continue."

'V.F Sorry, I couldn't resist. May I ask you why you have agreed to do this interview with us? This is a first, isn't it?

A.C I think you know the answer to that question.

V.F. *(I look blank.)* Err...actually...no.

A.C. My wife has bought your magazine.

V.F. She reads *Vanity Fair*?

A.C. I mean, literally. She has bought you. Out. She owns you now. Well, not you personally...*(he laughs).* The deal was sealed this morning. My wife, CEO of **HookedUp Enterprises**, is now your boss. She owns *Vanity Fair.*

V.F. So **HookedUp Enterprises** is not part of the Google buy-out?

A.C. No, its not, it's a separate entity. But you'd have to ask my wife the details. She's the businessperson now. I'm just her dogs-body. You know...around to make her a coffee if need be, hand out a bit of advice if she asks me. I'm going to be a kept man from now on. *(The curve of his lips makes me know he is being ironic.)*

V.F. Somehow I doubt that very much! So what will you do with all your spare time?

A.C. We've had a beautiful tree house built for us in a jungle in Thailand. It's hidden away in complete privacy on a private island. The jungle's surrounded by the ocean. I like to cook, you know, simple stuff like fresh fish I've caught that day, and Pearl reads novels. Meanwhile the twins putter about collecting seashells.

V.F. That sounds extremely romantic.

A.C. Romance is what gets me out of bed every day. Romance is what makes the world go round. Without romance one might as well not breathe.

V.F. So you and your wife are very in love?

A.C. I speak for myself when I say yes, absolutely. Now what's going on in that pretty head of Pearl's is anybody's guess.'

Pearl stopped reading and tittered to herself. She put down the magazine. "I thought I was an open book."

"Not at all," I said. "Sometimes you play it cool and I have no idea what you're thinking."

"I wear my heart on my sleeve—it's *you* who has everyone guessing. You're the trickster. You made me believe that it was over between us that time at Anthony's when I was blubbering in his back yard and you gave me all those 'goodbye' gifts. Bastard. Is there still a Coke in the cooler?"

"Coming right up," I said, snapping the ring, pouring the brown liquid into a glass and handing it to her. "Oh wait, let me give you some ice cubes. And a squeeze of lemon." I dressed up her drink and took a sip. "Delicious. Finish the article."

She squinted her eyes at me. "Why have you got a guilty look on your face?"

I took in a deep breath. Sometimes there are things that niggle your subconscious, even when your conscious mind has wiped it clean. This was one of those things. "Because there's something I never told you," I said tentatively. "Something I hid from you." The blood drained from Pearl's face. "Don't panic," I added, "it's nothing terrible—I'd even forgotten all about it, but when you mentioned the 'goodbye' gifts and so on; it came back to me."

She sat up. "Okay, come clean."

"I still have your old handbag. The one I told you was stolen. The old iPhone I smashed in a temper when I heard Laura's sneaky message telling you that Sophie was going to bump you off."

She raised an insolent brow. Uh oh, the whole Laura topic was about to be dragged out of the muddy mire. But Pearl answered coolly, "I know. When I was looking for an extra suitcase last year, I found the old purse stashed inside, at the back of one of your closets." She winked at me.

"How come you never let on?"

"Because I enjoyed having the last laugh. I loved the idea that you thought you had me out-foxed but, in fact, it was the other way round." Her lips tilted into a self-satisfied smirk, then she closed her eyes and lay back down. "Besides I got a forty grand Birkin bag out of it, so how could I complain?"

"How do you know it cost that much?" I asked. "You weren't meant to know the price!"

"The second Laura and her antennae saw the unusual color of the bag, she knew it was an one-off, custom-made piece of art. It was Laura, herself, who enlightened me; that dreaded time when I went to her house in London to confront her."

Please don't remind me of Laura. I squeezed Pearl's thigh. "So you weren't pissed at me, then, for holding out on you? For not being honest?"

"It was…what, a year later? Laura was dead. You were mine and everything had worked out just as it should have, so no. I was mildly miffed, but not angry. In fact, you probably did the right thing under the circumstances."

"You minx," I said, kissing her hand, "hiding all your inside knowledge."

"It takes two to tango, Chevalier." She opened her eyes—as blue as the ocean before us—and grinned.

"And we tango so beautifully together."

"Yes, we do. Speaking of finding stuff, I forgot to tell you. I found my great grandmother's diary in a box of my mother's that I had in storage."

I remembered Pearl telling me about her. She was a lady's maid, had an affair with the lord of the manor, and they ended up fleeing to America. "The racy one?" I asked. "The English one who eloped with the duke?"

She took a sip of her Coke. "That was pretty scandalous stuff in 1923."

"So what did the diary say?"

"I haven't read it yet. I'm savoring it for when I'm holed up in the hospital, giving birth."

"I doubt you'll be able to concentrate on reading, chérie. Remember the labor pains last time? The *last* thing you'll want to do is read."

"Funny how women have amnesia after giving birth. How we forget the horrible part of it."

"You were designed that way on purpose. If you remembered what a rough time of it you had, you might not go through with it again."

"You're right.

"Finish reading me the article," I said.

Pearl picked up the magazine again and leafed through it until she found the right page:

'Just as I am preparing my next question, a woman comes up to our table. At first, I think it is Charlize Theron (No surprise there, so many famous people stay at the George V.) But then I see it is none other than Pearl Chevalier, herself. She is stunning. Even more beautiful in the flesh than in photos. Her skin smooth and golden, her eyes a sparkling blue/gray. Her blonde hair is pinned up in a messy chignon and she's wearing a loose, flowing,

floral coat that looks as if it might be vintage Christian La-
croix. I notice her swollen belly. It is evident that Pearl
Chevalier is pregnant again.

Very pregnant indeed.'

"Sounds as if she had a crush on *you*, more like," I teased.

"Charlize Theron? Well, that *is* flattering, I have to admit"

"You're more beautiful than any movie star."

Pearl adjusted her weight, trying to find a comfortable position to accommodate her taut, round belly. "Love the touch
about the jungle. I don't think a jungle is quite my scene. Something Elodie might like, though. Have you heard from her lately?"

"She sent me an e-mail. What I said about hooking up with a
surfer? Guess what? She has. His name's Lucho and he's Colum-
bian," I told Pearl.

"From the frying pan into the fire."

"I don't think so—he sounds like a nice guy. He's only twen-
ty-three, or so. No money, just his surfboard and a good heart."

"Good luck to her, dating a surfer—if he's anything like my
dad."

"He sounds very committed to her. He has no idea who Elodie is, either." The words flew out of my mouth and I stopped.
*No idea who Elodie is...*Who *was* Elodie? Not even I had the
answer to that question.

"You mean, he has no idea she has a control-freak, powerful,
billionaire mother and an uncle who pretends he lives in a tree-
house in Thailand?"

"She's just a student with a backpack as far as he's concerned."

Pearl let the magazine drop onto the sand and stretched her

arms out. "Smart girl. Or she'd end up paying for his lodging and food for the next few months."

"I don't know—it sounds as if he's very keen on her."

"Well, anything's better than Mikhail Prokovich. I still can't believe he got his slimy hands on her. By the way, any more news on him? It seems so odd what happened. I just don't *get* how someone can kill themselves that way...surely survival instinct kicks in at the last moment?"

"Karma," I answered quickly. "It was meant to be. He got his just desserts."

"After all that work Natalie and I did," Pearl mumbled.

"Yeah, but you still exposed all his aides; all those dodgy people in high places who were making a mint because of the loopholes in the law."

"True." Pearl pondered what I'd said. "Alexandre, can I ask you a favor?"

I hesitated, hoping the conversation wouldn't go any further. "Sure. Anything."

"Will you rub some sunscreen on my back? I want to turn over." *Phew,* I thought. She maneuvered her body so she was now lying on her front, taking care to not squish her tummy.

"I'll try," I said, getting the cream out of her beach bag.

"What do you mean, you'll *try?*"

"Tall order," I said, squeezing some onto my palm and edging up to her towel. I placed my gooey hands over her shoulders and started to massage her smooth back. Within seconds I was as solid as a rod. I wanted to fuck here there and then. "Jesus, what is it about your skin?"

She turned her head; her eyes scanning down to the bulge in

my swim shorts and laughed, her teeth bright against her tan. She rolled over onto her back again, exposing her swollen belly once more. "Okay, do my tummy then if it's getting you so horny."

But her stomach didn't deter my ardor. Her pregnancy really turned me on. I began to rub the cream in gently—my eyes straying to her beautiful, big, full breasts. My cock started pounding; throbbing with desire. "I have to fuck you, Pearl. Please don't torment me with this." I leaned into her face and kissed her. "Please, chérie, let's go inside for a while. It's siesta time."

She looked over to where the nanny was making sandcastles with the twins, and sighed. "Poor Joy, we can't just abandon her."

I straddled her, my swim shorts tented with my raging hard-on. "Yes we can." I leaned down and breathed Pearl in. Sun. Coca Cola, sun cream, the Pearl Elixir. My eyes were hooded with lust. "I have to fuck you," I whispered into her ear, "but first I'm going to flicker my tongue between your legs and in every orifice you have—sweep my tongue all over you—make you scream out my name."

"Sold," she said. "But not here in public."

"That fast? Boy, that was easy."

"Well, what can I tell you, Alexandre Chevalier? I'm an easy lay."

I laughed, our lips touching "Not usually," I murmured into her mouth. "I have to earn my time with you these days."

"Let's go inside. I've had too much sun, anyway, for one day. I'll just let Joy know."

Our house was vast, a restored British colonial with polished wood floors, beamed ceilings, wood-lined walls and multiple, large, shuttered doors. From the ocean side we could whalewatch early in the mornings over a cup of coffee, observe the great creatures dive and splash in sun-glinted waves. Or from the bedroom upstairs, listen to the morning tweet of birds, and catch the view of both the sea and Salinas—there used to be a burgeoning salt industry here once—as sensual, tropical trade winds breezed through the open windows, always keeping us cool. I remembered the year before, trudging through the snow in Central Park, desperate to reunite myself with Pearl whom I feared I'd lost—longing for fatherhood and to start a family with her, and now here we were together. Parents. Basking in the warmth of family love, with another one on the way.

I was the luckiest man alive.

"Lie on the bed, Pearl, I'll continue that back massage I started." She'd just come out of the shower, naked, her golden tan glistening wet, her blonde hair dripping over her shoulders.

"I never say no to one of your massages." She lay herself gently on the bed, less able every day to lie on her stomach. "Even though you know I want a whole lot more than just a rub down."

With her on her front, I straddled her without putting any weight on her and began to knead her shoulders gently. It was tempting to fuck Pearl straight away but I got a thrill out of making her so relaxed, so wet, that by the time we had sex she was practically in tears she was so horny. In the past week, her pregnancy hormones had her wanting me more than ever.

"That feels wonderful," she groaned. "Just amazing."

I traced the tips of my fingers along her spine and down to the crack of her smooth ass, cupping her curves, massaging her buttocks. "This is a part of the body that gets ignored so often," I said. "It needs attention." I explored my fingers around her little dimples in the curve of her lower back, bent down and whispered kisses all over her. "I love you, baby," I told her, my breath hot on the nape of her neck.

"When you say 'baby', do you mean me or…we still haven't come up with a name, have we?"

"I mean both of you," I replied, drawing a slow circle around her dimples as I felt my cock stiffen up against my abdomen. "Don't worry, the perfect name will come at the perfect time."

"I need to turn over now," Pearl said in a bossy voice.

"Not yet, just relax." I trailed my hand down her back again, enticingly, as my fingers crept between her thighs. She was already soaked—I tapped her lightly there.

"Oh God," she moaned. "I need you to fuck me. Now."

"Sshh, chérie, I'm going to take my sweet time."

"Please, Alexandre, I need you inside me."

"Like this," I said, slipping my finger into her liquid heat, and sliding it out again.

"Oh please, don't torture me."

I tasted her on my finger. Delicious. I rolled her body over so she was on her back and pulled her down the bed. She loved being manhandled by me, loved it when I took control of her. I had her so she was on the edge of the bed, her legs dangling over, almost touching the floor. I nudged her thighs wide apart and got down on my knees. First, I kissed her inner thighs so lightly, knowing that all she could think about was her core; but I wanted to give her lots of anticipation. Then I leisurely stroked her glistening pussy up and down with my tongue, tasting her delectable nectar, darting it every now and then at her clit, then circling it. She was writhing and meowing.

"This is incredible. I love you, Alexandre. Oh God."

I always knew when Pearl was being driven wild because she brought God into her moaning pleas. It amused me. I slid my thumb inside her and continued with my tongue, pressuring it on her clit, hooking my thumb so it rested on her G-spot, moving it in a circular motion. She bucked her hips at me—she was in a blissful stupor. Keeping my thumb inside her, I moved my face away and turned my attention to one of her hard nipples and sucked. Jesus it made me horny. My dick was pounding. A low growl emanated from my throat. The feral sound made her grip my head and run her fingers passionately through my hair.

"I'm so wet, you're driving me crazy, Alexandre. Please fuck me."

"You want me to fuck you?" I teased, a smile tipping the corners of my mouth.

"Please...oh God, please. I need you inside me."

I pulled her back up the bed so she was more comfortable and took in my view. My woman with her swollen stomach. My seed, which was growing daily into a special being. "You're beautiful," I told her. "You've never been more beautiful."

She spread her legs even wider and I licked my lips—her pussy was like a split open fig—ripe and lush, smelling of the sun. I wanted to taste it again—go down on her once more. She notice my gaze, fixed between her legs.

She whispered, "I know what you're thinking but I need you inside me, baby—I need your lips on my lips, your breath on mine, your chest against my breasts; I need you close so there's no space between us."

Her words made me shudder. I lay over her; my weight

propped up by my elbows, and dipped my broad crown into her wetness. She cried out. She flung her arms about my shoulders and gripped me with her thighs, raising her hips and hooking her ankles around my ass. I felt myself plunge into her velvet warmth and I groaned like a wild animal, thrusting, sliding deeply back and forth—our worlds united as one.

"I. Love. Fucking. You. Pregnant," I rasped, now tantalizing her with mini thrusts, as I rammed my crown along her clit, over and over, her erotic zones stroked and stoked by my thick cock. She slid her tongue into my mouth and sucked on my tongue, ravenous for every part of me. She couldn't get close enough. I plunged in deeper, really fucking her now as her silk walls clamped around me.

"You feel amazing," I said, her kiss devouring my words. And she did. Pearl had a mélange of sweet innocence, coupled with raw sexuality; a heady cocktail that always sent me spinning. I had never been loved so much by anyone. Ever. My heart was thumping with love—waves of it crashing into her and leaving me breathless. I was weak with tenderness. But my aura was also on fire—light and heat circling our bodies like a parade of invisible angels looking on. Pearl had summoned God earlier with her cries, and a Higher Power—the Light—a Divine Flow, whatever you want to call it—was with us.

Everywhere.

I'm not a religious person, but if I had died in that moment I could have gone to my grave knowing, and having lived the ultimate definition of Paradise, because when Pearl and I climaxed together we lived inside one another's bodies for an instant. It is hard to explain, but it was a gift.

A parting gift to make what was about to shock our world, easier to bear.

19

The Bahamas boasts some of the best diving in the world, but of course Pearl couldn't do that, being pregnant. She was able to snorkel, though, and was happy working from her laptop, being mom, and reading novels.

I, however, took advantage of the incredible underwater world here. There are seven hundred different islands and cays but just forty-nine inhabited ones, so the place is replete with marine life, including dolphins, black tipped sharks, rays, and turtles, with protected, dropping reefs, deep as cliffs. It is a veritable diver's paradise and that was one of the reasons Pearl and I came here. We both needed a break from city life and I had been longing to really explore. We hired a cook and had Joy to help look after the twins, so we were incredibly spoiled and enjoying every minute of our extended vacation.

The early morning dive brought a plethora of underwater creatures going about their business. A Caribbean reef shark came alarmingly close to my flippers but swerved off in another direction. I saw spotted eagle rays, hawksbill turtles, an enormous grouper with its unhappy, turned-down mouth, and horse-eyed jacks in glittering silvery-blue with phosphorescent yellow-green fins, and all sorts of other brightly-colored tropical fish that I didn't know the names of. Fish—disguising themselves as sand, fish—in glaring yellow or with orange spots. I felt bad for a Lionfish, its red and gold stripes shimmering in the rays of the sun which were penetrating the deep blue of the water, because any second now, the other diver who had accompanied me would spear or net it and it would end up on somebody's plate. Through no fault of its own, this Lionfish was born into the wrong sea— not indigenous to these waters, its ancestors having made their way from the eastern coast of Africa to a Miami pet shop. Some blame it on the owners tossing them into the ocean when they started devouring their other fish in the tank, and others on Hurricane Andrew in 1992, smashing an aquarium tank, letting them loose. Here the creature was now, its dagger-sharp, venomous spines creating a sort of mane—an exquisitely beautiful specimen, condemned to death because it was threating the ecosystem here, an invasive species, feeding on juvenile reef fish and threatening the population of scores of marine creatures.

The water felt like silk against my skin, and it would have been easy to stay here all day but I wanted to get back to Pearl and the twins. I didn't want to become a dive-nerd. I'd seen some people suffer from that—so obsessed, they left their real lives behind. I'd left Pearl sleeping and promised (a whisper in her ear) that I'd be back before lunchtime. She groaned quietly with a little smile on her lips which both said, *Leave me to sleep and shut-up* and, *I love you.* Which, I wasn't sure, but then she did mumble, *Love you, babe,* so I went out feeling buoyed by the perfection in my life.

Those were her last words.

I came home from the dive, my head full of excitement with all I'd seen, bursting to relay all of it to my family, but as I walked up to the front door, Joy rushed towards me, her hand covering her face in panic. My instant reaction was that something had happened to one of the twins.

"Mr. Chevalier, it just happened five minutes ago. She was fine, just fine and then—"

"What? What's wrong? The babies?"

"No, your wife. I tried calling you but your cell was off. I've alerted the doctor—maybe Pearl had a sort of seizure. I called the doctor," she repeated.

"Well done." I rushed inside and Pearl was lying on the sofa stretched out, her lids closed, her face alarmingly pale— compared to the healthy-looking, tanned girl this very morning. My heart started hammering—fear and adrenaline spiked through my body into my fingertips, numbing me. "What the fuck is going on?" *My Pearl....my belle Pearl...*

"She's not responding but her heart's beating," Joy said, trembling. The cook was there with the children and everyone stared at me and then back to Pearl. I leaned down and felt Pearl's pulse. It was normal. Well, 'normal' wasn't the right word. Something was ominously wrong but I wasn't a medic so I had no idea what.

"What happened?" I demanded. Madeleine began to cry at the sound of my shrill voice. Joy swept my baby up into her arms

183

to placate her and said, "Pearl tripped and fell down, walking upstairs a few hours ago. Bumped the front of her head. Not long after you'd left. But she was fine. She even laughed about it afterwards. She didn't even have a cut. Nothing. Then about half an hour ago she said she had a headache and went to lie on the couch. I went to make her a cup of tea, I heard a sort of groan, and when I came back she was out. At first I thought she was sleeping, but she wouldn't wake up."

"Did she hurt her stomach when she fell?"

"No, I don't think so. She slipped and bashed her head but she didn't think it was anything to worry about."

I felt a shockwave of fury surge through my veins. Laura was fucking haunting us. First Elodie, miraculously being able to tie that sailor's knot and kill a man, and now Pearl, falling on the fucking stairs, repeating history. I could hear Laura now, manically laughing, thinking the whole thing was hilarious as she pulled her marionette strings from her armchair in Hell.

I looked at Joy. I was stumped. Horrified. *This isn't happening!* But not only was it happening, it had already fucking *happened.* "You called the doctor, you say?"

"She's on her way. Luckily, the number was on the fridge."

I smoothed my hand over Pearl's brow and noticed the swell of a bruise and discoloration there. It looked as if she had a concussion. I lifted her body up a touch to see if she'd react; if her muscles would clench, but she was as limp as a rag doll. She didn't stir. *Jesus, surely she couldn't be in a coma...could she?* I got out my cell.

"Pearl doesn't just need a doctor, she needs a fucking ambulance. No, she needs a helicopter." I called 911.

The next fifteen minutes were a blur. The doctor arrived, and while we waited for the helicopter, she took Pearl's blood pressure, pinched her nose, shone a light pen into her eyes and pricked her arm. No reaction from Pearl. The doctor confirmed the worst.

I heard Joy mumbling to herself, "Like that famous actress—what was her name? She tumbled while skiing on the beginner slopes—didn't have a bruise on her—she sent the medics away, saying she was fine. She die—"

I cut her off, "Pearl. Will. Be. Okay," I enunciated, glaring at her. "I can hear the helicopter now."

The medics rushed inside and laid Pearl on a stretcher. While they worked they asked us what had happened and words, overlapping, came tumbling out of our mouths at once; all of us trying to accept that what was taking place before our eyes was real. That was the irony of it all; a silly fall had gotten her into this unimaginable state. They always say accidents happen close to home but this was absurd! I had never seen Pearl so immoveable. Her skin was now looking marbled—it was as if they were about to carry away a valuable Greek statue that needed to be restored.

I put my hand on the shoulder of one of the paramedics to catch his attention—he was so involved in his task; putting an oxygen mask on Pearl, and then hooking her up to a drip, that it was an effort for him to even speak to me, let alone explain. All I knew by their manner, was that this was one hell of an emergency.

He said, "They'll need to access your wife's neurological status—her Glasgow Coma Scale to predict her ultimate outcome."

"What's normal?" I demanded.

"The score ranges from three to fifteen. Fifteen is normal, three is…" He didn't even finish his sentence.

Score—what a shit choice of words; as if someone in a coma had won something. "She's in a full-blown coma then?" I asked, double-checking. "This isn't just a temporary concussion?" I had been hoping that the doctor had somehow made the wrong diagnosis.

"Your wife has suffered head trauma and yes, she's in a coma."

"But it was just a silly fall!" I exclaimed, as if we could rewrite the past, as if my outburst could make a fucking difference.

"We're used to dealing with dive accidents, even golfing accidents, here in The Bahamas, but this really *is* unusual."

"Will the baby be okay?"

"I wouldn't like to say; they'll run tests."

At least he was being honest, although it was the last thing I needed to hear. "How can she be in a fucking coma from a little fall?" I persisted.

The medic adjusted Pearl's oxygen mask. "Often a person's immediate injury is not what does the most damage. More often than not, there's a secondary injury to the brain that can occur hours, even days, later. The patient, as in your wife's case, is unaware—may not even feel pain. Internal bleeding. That's why she suddenly had a headache."

I looked at him blankly. Not because I couldn't understand but because I felt as if I were floating through some surreal nightmare.

He took my vapid expression as miscomprehension and added, "The brain moves around in the skull, causing damage to nerve fibers and blood vessels. It causes the brain to swell which, in turn, blocks the flow of blood, causing tissue death."

Death. The word caused a rush of nausea to wash over me. "Not allowing oxygen to get to the brain?"

"Exactly, sir. That's why your wife is in a coma—it's the body's natural defense mechanism."

"So what now?"

"In all the cases I've seen like this, the patient needs intervention as soon as possible."

"Intervention?" My accent sounded more French than usual. Normal—I was out of my mind with fear.

"I'm 99% sure your wife's injuries are neurosurgical but the neurologist will determine her prognosis and the best course to take. Our job is to stabilize her and keep her alive until we get to hospital; I can't say what will happen next." *Keep her alive?* The reality was sinking in fast. If it weren't for them she might be dead by now, all from a goddamn stupid fall. *Things like this do not happen! Why pick on us for this freak-statistic-one-in-a-million kind of an accident?*

Before I could say another word, they rushed Pearl out through the doors to the helicopter, which was waiting on the lawn for them like a giant wasp, chopping up the wind.

I ran after them.

I had envisioned Pearl in the hospital—giving birth—but not this. I had been by her bedside now for ten hours straight. She'd been in OR and had come out still alive, so I was hopeful. Joy and the twins were in a hotel nearby.

The neurosurgeon—apparently one of the most talented in Miami, and even in the whole country, had done his best. Now all we could do was wait. I observed Pearl's face. She looked like a beautiful doll, although she had plastic tubes connected to her nose and mouth; the wheezing ventilator puffing in and out, ominously sounding like Darth Vader, feeding her oxygen, helping her breath, saving her *life*. Wires also ran all over the place and electrode pads on her chest, monitoring her heart. I stared at the green lines on the cardiac monitor in a trance.

I looked away and conjured up a vision of my Pearl, the Pearl who laughed so hard she'd wipe a tear from her face. Or scream at me the few times she got angry, or smother the babies in kisses from their heads to their toes, singing or chanting nursery rhymes. And then I'd look back at the statue of her. Still. Serious. Expressionless, and my eyes filled with burning tears.

Why? Why Pearl? Why not some schmuck who has it coming to him? Or someone who doesn't have the will to live? Why Pearl, of all people?

As I was wallowing in the injustice of it all, the nurse came by to give Pearl a sponge bath and set her IV pumps, saying she wanted to show me how to massage her. Up until now, I was scared of even touching her too much, as if by one wrong move I could cause her to stop functioning. The nurse had no extra news from the surgeons, other than that Pearl and the baby were 'stable' (e.g. alive). The neurologist, she assured, was on his way to talk to me. The last time we spoke, I hardly took in a word he said. All I knew was that Pearl had made it.

For now, anyway.

"Don't be nervous about massaging her," the young nurse insisted, as if reading my mind. "She's not made of glass."

But she is!

She took Pearl's slim arms in her fleshy brown hands and in a soothing voice said, "We need to keep her body supple so her muscles don't waste or her limbs might get locked into one position. It's important. The medical term is muscle atrophy—we don't want that to happen. Here, give me your hands." She took my large, awkward hands and placed them on Pearl's legs. "Go on, give her a good massage." But all I could do in that moment was bury my head in her thighs and weep. The Pearl Elixir had been replaced with a clinical, medical aroma—the odor of cleanliness and iodine, or whatever they used to swab her down with before she went into surgery.

"I'll be back in a minute," the nurse said discreetly, leaving me to my inner-turmoil.

I stayed that way for a good five minutes but then sat up with a jolt. *Get it together, Alexandre!* I believed that coma patients could feel and hear, despite what they told me, and I didn't want Pearl to sense my anguish.

Even though I rarely prayed and never went to church, I was brought up a Catholic and that shit sticks with you, whether you like it or not. Suddenly God was getting my undivided attention. I'd felt furious with Him (Her?) all day but I reckoned I needed to be a little more amenable if I were to receive any special favors.

So I took a big breath and prayed. I prayed my fucking heart out.

"Please bring Pearl and our beautiful baby back to me. I'll do anything you want."

Anything.

The neurosurgeon came by on his rounds, ten minutes earlier than I expected, and woke me up from a doze. He was cool, professional—a tall, almost gangly man, with a gentle stoop. I guessed he must have been about fifty. Although I knew he would have done everything possible, it unnerved me that this was just his day job. It wasn't his *life*. If Pearl didn't make it, he'd feel bad, would have tried his darned best, but it wouldn't *destroy his world*. I wanted everyone to feel my pain, my fear, my anguish. I wanted everyone here to be as invested in Pearl as I was. But when they got home after work, they had their own lives to lead, their own families and problems. Pearl was not their number one priority. They were mere human beings. What if someone fucked up?

My face was a mask as the surgeon explained the operation. How a substantial amount of blood was removed because the tissue had swelled against the inflexible bone. How they had to relieve the pressure inside the skull by placing a ventriculostomy drain to eliminate excess cerebrospinal fluid. He was trying to speak in layman's terms so I'd understand. I was grateful for that; right now my mind was holding too much fear to think coherently. He told me how they'd removed a tiny piece of skull to accommodate the swelling, which they'd re-implant at a later date. He talked about measuring pressure, inserting valves, and a dozen other medical procedures.

"What about the baby?" I asked. "Won't the anesthesia have harmed the baby?"

The man was calm. I didn't know whether to feel grateful for his cool, professional demeanor, or furious. Good, he was in control of the situation. Bad, he was dispassionate, as if Pearl were just another patient. Because, let's face it, she was...*just another patient* to him. His patients were his profession but were they *his world? His life?* His Universe would not come tumbling down if Pearl didn't live.

He looked down for a second, took a breath, looked me in the eye and then said succinctly, "Obviously, our first priority is with the mother, with Pearl, but there is no evidence that babies born to mothers who had surgery during pregnancy have a higher incidence of birth defects. We adjusted the dose accordingly— our anesthesiologist is the best in his field, don't worry. We're doing all we can." His last sentence spoke volumes. *We're doing all we can.* And I detected a glint of sympathy that flickered in his gaze. The last thing I fucking needed.

I looked away because I didn't want him to see that tear fall. The tear that told him I was almost a broken man. I turned from him, wiped my face and focused on a huge white bunch of lilies that Sophie had sent. The sweet cloying aroma was wafting about the room and for a second, it made me feel appeased. Pearl loved white lilies. Our engagement cake when I took her to the Empire State was garnished with fresh white lilies. She loved the smell of them, the elegant shapes they made.

I needed to be strong. For Pearl. For my children.

For myself.

20

I t was early in the morning when Daisy slipped into the hospital room as noiselessly as a cat burglar. I sat up from my recliner with a jolt. At first I didn't recognize her—she looked taller than before—but on a double take I noticed that she must have lost weight, and her extra height was just an illusion. Her fiery red hair had lost some of its wildness, too.

"I came as soon as I could," she whispered. Her eyes were swollen and red, her eyelids enflamed. But her expression now was brave and her attitude chirpy as if everything were quite normal. *Nice try, Daisy.* Still, I appreciated the effort.

"Billy's getting us some coffees from the vending machine."

I looked at her blankly. "Billy, Pearl's dad?"

"Yeah, he'll be here in five minutes."

"You came together?"

Daisy moved quietly over to Pearl's side and took her hand. "Yes, we flew from Hawaii." A tear slid down her English-rose cheek.

"Your living in Hawaii now?"

"Moved there a couple of months ago."

"Where's Amy?"

"With her dad in New York for a few days. You know, we're getting a divorce but it's still great for her to see him when she can." She managed a limp smile.

"You're living in Kauai?" I repeated, glad to have some distraction from my motor-mind. You came all this way?"

"Of course I did, Pearl's my best friend."

For the next five minutes, I told Daisy all I knew about Pearl's condition, rattling off, in a monotone, every piece of information I gleaned from the neurosurgeon. I was on automatic pilot, my sensations numbed, my body felt as if it were stuffed with cotton wool. The neurologist, who was working alongside the surgeon, had also given me an update, earlier this morning. Pearl was stable but there was no improvement. He didn't look hopeful, at all, but he wouldn't give anything away.

Daisy said brightly, "I've prepared an iPod for Pearl. All her favorite songs. I thought she could have a listen in between siesta time." We both tried to laugh at her joke but then she burst out crying and I tried not to let the lump in my throat morph into a full-blown sob. Daisy wept as we clung to each other, our bodies shaking, gripping each other for dear life, because that's what it was…what it *is…Dear Life*. Even when staring death in the face in the French Foreign Legion, I had never appreciated the fragility of life as I did in that moment.

A freak accident, tripping on the stairs—that's all it took for Pearl to be animated and extraordinary one minute, and the next, three hours later, a ghost of herself.

That is what life can do. Life can take away life from anyone, at any second. We cannot take it for granted. We cannot control it. We cannot expect it to dance to our tune.

I was looking at Pearl's ghost now and it terrified me, mainly because I felt responsible.

"I feel so guilty, Daisy. If only I hadn't had the stupid, fucking idea for us to go to the Caribbean. What a fool! We should have stayed in New York. Or Paris. Or somewhere that had state-of-the-art hospitals five minutes away, that didn't involve a fucking helicopter ride."

"We all know that's not true, Alexandre. Accidents can happen anywhere. *Catastrophes* can happen anywhere, even right on your doorstep. 9/11 is a perfect example of that. You cannot prepare yourself against Fate's cruel blows. If you live that way, you are only half a person."

"But I should have been more careful. I should—"

"It's not your fault, Alexandre. It was a freak accident. The damage occurred in the few hours between her fall and when she fell into a coma. Even if Pearl had been on the doorstep of any hospital in New York City, knowing her, she would have laughed it off and said she didn't need a doctor, that she felt fine. It was a one in a million thing. She was just fucking unlucky."

Her words were kind but didn't alleviate the hatred I felt for myself. All my fury I'd had the night before for the medical team, was now directed at myself. What kind of shit husband takes his family to a fucking island, when his wife is five months pregnant and his children are toddlers?

"I mean it wasn't as if you were in some third-world country," Daisy went on, as if she could read my thoughts. She pulled away from me and looked at me steadily in the eye. "The Bahamas are safe, Americanized. What happened to Pearl could have happened anywhere. Besides, it was her idea to go off to the Caribbean and take a long break."

"Yes, but she did it for me."

"Bollocks, Alexandre, she did it because she wanted to. Pearl is headstrong, she does what she wants." Daisy looked down at her feet. "Sorry, 'headstrong' wasn't the best choice of words."

I tried to smile. "Actually, it is the perfect word to describe Pearl and it gives me hope. She'll get through this, Daisy. I promise." I kissed Daisy's brow lightly and felt comfort with her being there; knowing she was going through the same sort of pain as I was. She could identify. She understood.

"I brought coffee and doughnuts." I looked up and saw Billy with a tray. He set it down on a table and came over to shake my hand. Then he laid an arm around Daisy's shoulder. Were they dating? Just friends? From the way she shifted her body a touch away from him, it looked as if he had one thing in mind and she another. He pointed to the coffees. "These two have cream. The other's black."

I took one of the paper cups. "I'll take the black one if that's okay."

"Pearl drinks black," Daisy said. "That song, *Black Coffee*—the All Saint's version, not the Julie London version, is on the mixed tape. On her iPod, I mean. I've tried to have mostly upbeat songs, you know. Perk her up a little. *Wake Up Little Suzy* is on there, too. Apparently, music can nudge people out of comas, especially if it's a song they recognize and that means something to them."

Perk her up? I looked at Pearl. *Sleeping Beauty.* Maybe I was enough of a French frog to get her to wake up if I kissed her. Or did she have to kiss me back?

Daisy wrung her fingers through her thick red hair. "I made a promise to her once and I'll need to speak to the staff about it."

"A promise?" I felt nervous. What kind of promise? *To get them to pull the fucking plug?* To donate her organs? My eyes were darts, but Daisy just shook her head and smiled.

"Don't look so horrified, Alexandre."

Funny, this woman can read my thoughts.

"Once, Pearl and I were joking around, and she made me swear that if she ever ended up in a coma or was a vegetable, unable to move, that I'd make sure her beauty regime was taken care of. You know, hair-care, leg waxing and stuff. It was a *joke*— I never thought it would actually bloody *happen*, but a promise is a promise."

I heaved a sigh of relief.

Silence sliced through the air like a razor. We looked at each other, Billy cast his eyes at the floor—maybe to stop himself from breaking down, and everybody felt speechless. Except Daisy started chatting again; obviously wanting to fill the awkward void.

She inhaled the bunch of flowers. "These lilies are beautiful. Pearl's favorite. Well, I guess you know that already or you wouldn't have chosen them."

"Sophie sent them," I said.

"How is Sophie?"

"Fine, she'll be here tomorrow," I told her.

"You sold HookedUp, then?"

"Yeah, we did." *Shut up with the small talk, Daisy.*

"Anthony's on his way, right?"

"Yes, he'll be here in a while."

"Oh God, I nearly forgot!" Daisy said, reaching into her purse. "The last time we saw Pearl she let Amy try on her pearl necklace, you know…Amy had been obsessing about it for over a year…so for a special treat, we let her, and wouldn't you know it, Amy went off with it! Naughty magpie."

Daisy carefully brought out the Art Deco necklace I had given Pearl—the lucky one with eighty-eight pearls, the number of infinity of the Universe, the number of constellations in the sky. She laid the necklace about Pearl's pale neck and fiddled with the diamond clasp for what seemed forever. I felt a lump choke up my throat.

"There…these pearls can work some magic, maybe," Daisy said, and then lowered her voice to a whisper, "The nurse will probably say she isn't allowed to wear them, or something, but worth a try, eh?"

The shimmering pearls looked exquisite, lustrous; myriad tones of pinkish gold and honey. I looked away—I thought I'd break into pieces.

"You know what?" I said, hardly able to speak. "I think Billy might want to be with his daughter for a bit. Have a chat." *Hint, hint, Billy—let Pearl know you're sorry for being such an absent father when she needed you most.* My anger was surging back again. At Billy, at myself. Pearl looked so beautiful in the necklace that I could no longer bear to look at her. I needed to get the hell out of this sterile hospital room for an hour or two so she didn't feel my negative vibe.

"I'm going to my hotel to clean up, have something to eat and see my kids," I told them. "I'll be back in a bit. You've all got my number. Call me if anything, you know…happens. I'm five minutes away."

Billy's tall frame stood and sadness was carved across his weather-beaten face. He was a handsome man, with his loose, sandy-blond hair, and looked younger than his fifty-something years. But right now he looked like shit. I guess we all did.

Being back with my children temporarily eased me somewhat. I lay on the floor, which was carpeted wall-to-wall in a thick wool pile, and let them crawl all over me as if they were puppies. I told them how much their mother doted on them and that there was another baby on the way, trying to convince myself that everything would work out fine. But I felt haunted by what Daisy told me; that Pearl had asked her to make sure her legs got waxed if she ended up in a coma. Did she have a premonition? Sometimes, a voice speaks to you. Your subconscious, your gut, your instinct—call it what you will. Perhaps Pearl *knew* this was going to happen.

I played airplane with Madeleine, which she adored, lying on my back and balancing her on my feet while holding her hands. Louis was more grounded. He didn't want to fly or play wild games. He wanted to be quiet and look at picture books or play with colored blocks.

"I've ordered room service," Joy said, standing at the doorway. I turned to look at her and saw she'd been crying too. We were all pretending to each other to be brave but inside we were mush. "I thought you needed some nourishment before you went back to the hospital." She retied her ponytail so her dark hair was scraped against her scalp. I'd become a bit obsessed with scalps, heads and brains in the last twenty-four hours. They'd shaved part of Pearl's head. With my babies, I was always so careful when I held them, afraid to drop them, but a grown woman, who would have known such a thing could happen?

"Great." I didn't even bother asking Joy what she'd ordered. I didn't care. Eating right now was an aid to help me function, nothing more. A way to fuel myself. The neurologist told me that they'd run more tests, but he didn't want to put my hopes up.

As well as talking to all the medical staff, I'd done research. That's all I did, in between massaging Pearl, reading her poetry and stories, and talking to her. But I hung on to Hope, Faith and fucking Charity. I reckoned for all the shit I went though for the first half of my life, I was owed one.

When I got back to the hospital, Anthony was there. He was dressed in a bright yellow shirt and pink pants, his head on Pearl's cheek, crying his heart out. Daisy had put the ear buds on Pearl and the iPod switched on. I thought I heard the tune, *Unchained Melody* and it made my eyes smart. Another nurse—an older woman, this time—waddled in, adjusted Pearl's IV bags, double-checked settings and the cardiac monitor, and left, leaving our motley party to get on with it.

Anthony didn't even notice me. Billy was quietly reading a

magazine. Daisy looked up at me, her eyes even more puffed than before, her mascara smudged. She took me aside and mouthed silently, "Bruce is also in the hospital. Anthony's freaking out."

"Bruce, his boyfriend?"

"He's had another aneurism. Obviously Anthony's torn in two. Guilty if he didn't come here, guilty now he *is* here. He'll be flying back to San Francisco on the red-eye."

"Poor guy. Any change in Pearl?" I whispered. I didn't want Pearl to hear us, even though they assured me she was out of it.

"Not a peep," Daisy murmured back. "And that's another reason why Ant is freaking out. He overheard one of the neurologists talking about Pearl's condition. But Ant is such a drama queen, I don't know."

"But I spoke to Dr. Bailey earlier. He said it's too soon to make a definitive prognosis—that we need to wait."

"That's what I hoped too. But they won't speak to me because I'm not family."

"You *are* family, Daisy."

"Thanks for that." She wiped a tear from her eye. "Anthony said that—"

"I heard the doctors discussing Pearl earlier," Anthony piped up, his lip trembling, his body shaking uncontrollably.

Billy put his magazine down and gathered a measured breath. "We need to speak to Dr. Bailey directly, Ant. What you heard was hearsay." His face was gaunt and drained, his eyes empty with fear.

I came over to Anthony and laid my hand on his shoulder and gave him a pat as if to say, *There, there, now.* I felt ridiculous—I didn't know what else to do—the man was a blubbering mess. I didn't want him to say anything in front of Pearl but he couldn't be stopped.

He blurted out, "They were talking in a lot of technical, medical jargon, you know. Cerebral edema, sub-something-or-other bleeding, cervical spine fracture. They said that her frontal lobes and parietal lobes are irreparably damaged, and that when the anesthesia wears off they can establish brain death. Something about Doppler flows and oh yes, of course they want to get their greedy hands on her kidneys." He started wailing, braying like a donkey, tears spilling from his inflated eyes. "Why me? Why is it all happening at once?" he yodeled.

I squeezed his shoulders. "No, Anthony. Dr. Bailey wouldn't be so unprofessional. He's one of the most respected neurosurgeons in the country. And the neurologist, too. They'd let us know something like that, straight away. There's the baby to think of, as well. You must have misheard."

Anthony gulped air. "It's the weekend. He probably wanted to go fishing or something…you know, couldn't face getting into some heavy family drama, so thought he'd wait until after the weekend to tell us the bad news."

I didn't want to argue about this with my brother-in-law, out of his mind with upset, so I let it pass. I had an urge to throttle Anthony, choke some sense into him, chuck them all out of the room, Daisy included, and just lie there quietly with Pearl. Alone. But they, too, had a right to be with her.

Yet Anthony continued, as he wrung and twisted his fingers through his hair and cried, "I'm sorry, call me a coward but I am *not* going to stay here and watch my sister die! I mean, she is dead, right? Technically *dead,* being kept alive by machines? Her brain isn't functioning!" His pale blond eyebrows shot up. "All they have to do is yank out the tubes and that'll be it!"

"Enough, Ant," Billy barked, trying to remain calm. His fists were clenched though; the tension in his body was raw, his Adam's apple bobbing in his throat, his jaw tense. "If you need to leave, then just go. Nobody is judging you—we all will deal with this on our own terms."

"That's right, Dad. And my terms are shattered to pieces! My terms are...fuck, I don't know...I can't even think straight, but I cannot and *will* not watch while they fucking pull that plug. Bruce needs me. Pearly isn't even aware that I'm here!"

"I dispute that," Daisy said quietly. "She knows. She knows in her soul and in her heart—which, even if her brain *is* supposedly... 'dead,' is still beating, by the way." She whispered the word dead. "She *knows,"* she added, "how much we love her." Daisy buried her face in her hands and then rushed out of the room, crying, into the corridor. I followed her, nearly crashing into a man hobbling along with an IV pole. I needed to find the nurse, call the doctor on his cell or find someone who knew what the fuck was going on.

Pearl's brain had to be alive and functioning. Who was to say someone was 'brain dead,' anyway? There were miracles, weren't there? Misdiagnoses? She *had* to pull through.

She just had to.

Or I'd wander through life nothing better than a grain of dust.

PEARL'S EPILOGUE.

His hands were music to me all day long. His touch so full of love, so perfect, that I drifted in and out of a blissful dream. We were making love and he was telling me that I was the most beautiful woman he had ever known. Were we making love? I don't know, because every time I woke up it was just the movement of his hands and the song of his voice. Poetry. Stories. Tales of Madeleine and Louis. Laughter filled my ears.

And here I am. In a strange world of non-being, yet feeling so alive! So alive with love. I've lived. I've done everything I've ever wanted to do. Some people will tell you that living is the most important thing. But I say it's true only if you are living with life in your *heart*. Otherwise you're dead.

I can feel myself drifting away to *Utopia*. I don't care that I'm leaving Life behind. Because I have loved. I'm in love and have *been* loved. And nobody can ever take that away from me. Someone special—Alexandre—has given me his all. I am full. Literally.

I see a light and it's smoothing itself all around me like a warm sea. I'm bathed in shimmering gold luminosity. I'm weightless, floating. I can see Mom and she's laughing.

She's beckoning me to join her, calling my name.

ALEXANDRE'S EPILOGUE.

Six months later.

The memorial went beautifully, thanks to Ant who organized it all. White lilies adorned the little church on the hill and the view below was breathtaking. Rolling hills and green valleys patch-worked over the land, with houses dotted here and there. I knew that Pearl loved countryside like this. Her dad stood there, his hands behind his back, standing tall and proud, and I wondered if he minded that Daisy hadn't chosen him, after all.

Louis and Madeleine were scampering about, squealing with delight. Only children have the privilege of being so uncouth; blissfully unaware of the turmoil going on in grown-ups' heads, I thought. But Ant had been brave today and hardly shed a tear. The pastor read some lovely prayers and Anthony read a Walt Whitman poem—one of Pearl's favorites, in fact.

I was wearing a suit, the same one that I'd worn on our wedding day. I felt a lump in my throat, remembering the beauty of the falling snowflakes, Pearl's exquisite face, and I was grateful to have that memory—indeed *all* the memories of our wonderful life together.

I felt an arm slip under my jacket and snake it's way around my waist. I looked down at my wife. "So, what did you think?"

"I'm sure Bruce would have loved this," she said.

"Well, I never met the man, but the service was beautifully done."

I peered down into the carrycot just to check on little Lily. Her smooth, delicate face looked so peaceful and her heart-shaped, pouting lips so content.

"Don't worry, she'll be asleep for a while now," Pearl said, nestling her head against my shoulder.

"Shall we go back to the hotel and make another?" I asked with a crooked smile.

"Another baby? You're a fast worker, Alexandre Chevalier; I think I'm babied-out for a good long while. But if you're *careful*, I guess—"

"Let's go back, right now. I feel like hanging out with only you, all afternoon."

"What about those two rascals?" Pearl said gesturing over to our two runaround tornadoes on the loose.

"Joy," I said, "is not called Joy for nothing. She can take them to see the Golden Gate."

"You're on," Pearl agreed.

"That easy?"

"I told you I was an easy lay," she said, and laughed.

"I wish," I answered, taking all of her in my arms. I squeezed her tight and breathed in the Pearl Elixir. "For forty-eight whole hours I thought I'd lost my rare Pearl," I murmured into her soft blonde hair. "My belle Pearl."

Yes, those couple of days when Pearl was in a coma was the worst time of my life. But it turned out that the conversation between doctors that Anthony overheard was about another patient altogether, not Pearl. It was a good thing he returned home to Bruce, because Bruce died two days later. His family organized the funeral, negating the fact that Anthony was his boyfriend—refusing to have anything to do with him at all, so Anthony got this memorial together, six months later. We were now all saying goodbye. It was a poignant moment for me because, although it was sad, I couldn't help but feel that one life was lost and another gained.

Pearl survived.

Daisy was right. *Wake Up Little Suzy* jolted Pearl out of the coma. Her recovery was not immediate, obviously. It took her a long time to get back to complete normality and she spent most of that time in the hospital, due to her pregnancy. I didn't want to take any risks. But the birth went beautifully and she hardly suffered any labor pains, this time around. When little Lily popped out completely healthy, with all her fingers and toes, I thought I'd burst, I was so happy.

Since then, Pearl and I have been taking it easy. With HookedUp out of our lives and more money than anyone needs for several lifetimes, we don't have to work. Natalie has taken over HookedUp Enterprises, and Pearl just acts as consultant once in a while. She sold on *Vanity Fair*—she realized that running a magazine was very different from reading one—in fact, she spends a lot of time reading, and is working on a book based on her great-grandmother's journals. She's a full-time mom and I'm a full-time househusband. The best job I've ever had. After the scare—thinking I had lost Pearl forever—I realized that there is nothing more important than family. Nothing.

Even Sophie has chilled out. After the Google buy-out, she saw the digits of her bank account and nearly fainted. She decided to take a year off and travel around Europe with Alessandra. (Who was nominated for an Oscar for *Stone Trooper* but didn't win.) Sophie finally got a divorce, and her husband married his mistress: a young woman who had been his personal assistant. What a cliché.

All my exes finally accepted that Pearl was the only woman for me and they gave up their pursuit. Indira even sent flowers to the hospital when Pearl came out of her coma, and Claudine sent her a get-well card. Other than that, everything trundles along as it was, except Sally has her hands full with three dogs; we kept one of Rex and Bonnie's puppies. People still believe Bonnie's collar is made of real diamonds.

As for Elodie, she's still traveling about South America, searching for her vocation in life. I have a feeling she has a long and fascinating story to tell. Time will tell. She's a dark horse, that one.

And as for us? Pearl and I have never been happier. I treasure each moment that we have together, each second, each minute, each hour.

We are inseparable.

Thank you so much for coming along on Pearl and Alexandre's emotional journey with me. I owe so much to you, my readers, and without you none of this would have happened.

I have more stories to tell, and I hope you will come along for the ride. So please sign up (ariannerichmonde.com/email-signup) to be informed the minute any future Arianne Richmonde releases go live. Your details are private and will not be shared with anyone. You can unsubscribe at any time.

I have also written *Glass*, a short story.

Join me on Facebook
https://www.facebook.com/AuthorArianneRichmonde

Join me on Twitter
https://twitter.com/A_Richmonde

For more information about me, visit my website.
http://ariannerichmonde.com/

If you would like to email me:
ariannerichmonde@gmail.com

Belle Pearl Playlist

Un Homme et Une Femme – Francis Lai

Lady Grinning Soul – David Bowie

California Girls – The Beach Boys

Je ne Regrette Rien – Edith Piaf

Royals – Lorde

Skyfall – Adele

You Really Got Me – The Kinks

Cello concerto in D Minor – Vivaldi

Black Coffee – All Saints

Unchained Melody – Righteous Brothers

Utopia – Gold Frapp

Wake Up Little Suzy – Everly Brothers

To listen to the soundtrack, go to:
http://ariannerichmonde.com/music/belle-pearl-sound-track/

23485275R00124

Made in the USA
Middletown, DE
29 August 2015